As AI becomes a part of everyday life across every industr concise voice like Sarah's is desperately needed. Her work gets to the core of the issue whilst providing both newcomers and enthusiasts a bridge to understanding this critical technology.

Russ Shaw CBE, Founder of Tech London Advocates and Global Tech Advocates

The new edition of Sarah Burnett's book provides an essential roadmap through the rapidly-developing landscape of AI technology and services. Sarah provides a clear-eyed view of, as she says in the book, 'the opportunities we are gaining and the risks we are facing'. The case studies in particular will be essential reading for those seeking to understand the challenges and potential of AI for their own organisations. Highly recommended.

Audrey Mandela, Chair, Women in Telecoms and Technology (WiTT)

This book is a must-read for anyone wanting to stay ahead in AI. It provides a thorough view of AI's current and future impact on business and innovation, with practical examples and detailed case studies that illustrate the concepts. The new edition is particularly noteworthy, as it includes updates on the latest developments in AI, such as generative AI and agentic AI, making it an invaluable resource for business leaders looking to embrace the future to drive their organisations forward. Its practical insights and real-world examples make it an essential guide for anyone looking to harness the power of AI in their business growth strategy.

Dr. Adam Bujak, CEO, KYP.ai

I appreciate the way Sarah writes about AI in a clear and relevant way. This updated edition covers what you need to know that matters, in particular the new case studies show how AI can drive real competitive advantage for any enterprise.

Andrew Anderson, Technology Chairman and Investor

Masterful insight, this book is more relevant than ever. It is critical reading for the business leaders of today and tomorrow. Through many illustrations and case studies, learn how AI is inevitable for your business to boost innovation, efficiency, and for it to become autonomous!

Pascal Bornet, Author of 'Intelligent Automation'

In this updated version of the book, the author advances the real, practical examples that help illustrate the spectrum from possibility to current reality. The focus on enterprise use cases is particularly helpful to business executives wanting to calibrate their thinking on what AI can and will mean for their enterprise.

Eric Simonson, Managing Partner, Everest Group

Reviews on previous edition:

Burnett offers a comprehensive foundation and directional understanding of the future of business in this book. Her years of analyses into the world of technology shines through, as she explains the current state of artificial intelligence being used across the world of business and why you should get involved. She weaves a series of exciting case studies, from a wide range of examples to bring to life a story of potential for the companies and individuals involved at this evolutionary initial step towards an autonomous enterprise. A must read.

Rob Hughes, Co-founder and CEO, Techopian

I recommend this book for executives who need a business-focused primer on AI and the opportunities that it brings for innovation and efficiency. The book explains AI and intelligent automation as the next set of innovation levers driving business results in leading enterprises. Executives will learn the language of intelligent automation, including the major classes of tools, their capabilities, and limitations, and how they work together. Sarah Burnett's book addresses implementation challenges and the practices that delivered business value in real-world case studies.

Mary Lacity, Walton Professor of Information Systems at the University of Arkansas, Co-author of 'Becoming Strategic with Robotic Process Automation'

Essential reading for all business decision makers who need to understand the basics and future possibilities. The book provides an insightful and comprehensive coverage of the current world of AI, explaining how it is a business enabler, provides increased opportunities for innovation and efficiency. Sarah Burnett's case studies demonstrate the positive impact AI has already had and that investing in AI is necessary as it continues modernising and disrupting the tech industry.

Andrea Palmer FBCS, Chair BCS Women and Consultant, Infosys Consulting

Will intensify your AI curiosity. It is filled with wonderful examples of humans and machines working together and learning. Sarah uses AI for good, ethically driven, to build the Autonomous Enterprise with concepts such as phygital. It makes AI relevant to us all in a style that relates to everyone.

Andrew Lowe, Co-author of the BCS publication 'Artificial Intelligence: Learning From Experience'

AI IN BUSINESS

BCS, THE CHARTERED INSTITUTE FOR IT

BCS, The Chartered Institute for IT, is committed to making IT good for society. We use the power of our network to bring about positive, tangible change. We champion the global IT profession and the interests of individuals, engaged in that profession, for the benefit of all.

Exchanging IT expertise and knowledge
The Institute fosters links between experts from industry, academia and business to promote new thinking, education and knowledge sharing.

Supporting practitioners
Through continuing professional development and a series of respected IT qualifications, the Institute seeks to promote professional practice tuned to the demands of business. It provides practical support and information services to its members and volunteer communities around the world.

Setting standards and frameworks
The Institute collaborates with government, industry and relevant bodies to establish good working practices, codes of conduct, skills frameworks and common standards. It also offers a range of consultancy services to employers to help them adopt best practice.

Become a member
Over 70,000 people including students, teachers, professionals and practitioners enjoy the benefits of BCS membership. These include access to an international community, invitations to a roster of local and national events, career development tools and a quarterly thought-leadership magazine. Visit www.bcs.org to find out more.

Further information
BCS, The Chartered Institute for IT,
3 Newbridge Square,
Swindon, SN1 1BY, United Kingdom.
T +44 (0) 1793 417 417
(Monday to Friday, 09:00 to 17:00 UK time)
www.bcs.org/contact

https://shop.bcs.org/
publishing@bcs.uk

www.bcs.org/qualifications-and-certifications/certifications-for-professionals/

AI IN BUSINESS
Towards the autonomous enterprise
Second edition

Sarah Burnett

Published by BCS Learning and Development Ltd, a wholly owned subsidiary of BCS, The Chartered Institute for IT, 3 Newbridge Square, Swindon, SN1 1BY, UK.
www.bcs.org

Paperback ISBN: 978-1-78017-6673
PDF ISBN: 978-1-78017-6680
ePUB ISBN: 978-1-78017-6697

Ebook available

British Cataloguing in Publication Data.
A CIP catalogue record for this book is available at the British Library.

Publisher's acknowledgements
Reviewers: Eric Jukes, Karthik Ravichandran, Kay Hardy
Publisher: Ian Borthwick
Commissioning editor: Heather Wood
Production manager: Florence Leroy
Project manager: Sunrise Setting Ltd
Copy-editor: Gillian Bourn
Proofreader: Graham Frankland
Indexer: John Silvester
Cover design: Alex Wright
Cover image: iStock - piranka
Sales director: Charles Rumball
Typeset by Lapiz Digital Services, Chennai, India

CONTENTS

LIST OF FIGURES AND TABLES

ABOUT THE AUTHOR

Sarah Burnett is a renowned technology industry analyst and international speaker who advises enterprises on intelligent automation, ethical uses of technology, competitive strategies and market trends. She helps intelligent automation technology vendors successfully formulate their product direction, go to market strategies, and apply ethical policies.

She gained a Bachelor of Science degree in physics and electronics and a Master's degree in applied optics from Reading University in 1981 and 1982, respectively, and has worked in the computer industry ever since, the last 10 years in the field of intelligent automation.

Sarah is a strong advocate for women in technology. She chaired BCS Women for four years and continued to work with the group as chair of AI Accelerator, which she founded in 2017, until 2022. AI Accelerator was a programme of free AI events by experts, to inform participants and make AI accessible to more people.

Sarah is a Fellow of BCS.

FOREWORD

'AI' has always been long on rhetoric and striking examples, and short on what is mostly, really, happening in our organisations. For a long time now Sarah Burnett has provided seasoned objective, detailed and valuable insight on automation and digitalisation, and has always been one of the few analysts you go to automatically to find out what is happening, and what is going to happen. This is the long-awaited book. It draws on an impressive knowledge hinterland thoroughly wrung from the author's roles as researcher, practitioner and analyst. She has spent much time engaging with and thinking through myriad examples across sectors and the globe. She has always been incredibly up to date. Unsurprisingly, this is a distinctive feature of the book. An introductory chapter – alone worth the price of the volume – offers a detailed overview explaining the concept of the autonomous enterprise, and many examples spread across retail, finance and healthcare.

The book then gives a very comprehensive and detailed analysis of what 'AI' amounts to. I have always found this a task best compared to hacking one's way through a conceptual jungle full of strange noises and false trails. The author does an outstanding job of making the vocabulary consistent and usable, and the area understandable. With the jungle behind us, there are then relatively sunlit uplands in the form of a compelling assessment, using many illustrations, of how these technologies are already being used to achieve innovation and efficiency, and much more besides.

Reading these chapters, we become aware that the potential is massive, that imagination and disciplined management are required, and that an enormous amount of value is still being left on the table. Four enlightening case studies follow, and these ground our understanding in the management realities of organisational functioning. Having written a few case studies in my time, I can say that these are exceptional in spelling out the vision needed, the preparatory work, the investment, the organisational challenges and the sheer hard work required.

While many talk of fast digital transformation, and the imminent arrival of digital business, this book posits no overnight successes, rather a slow evolution, with automation at the heart of things. The view of the autonomous enterprise is distinctive and convincing. Automation changes how things are done in the enterprise. For example, it turns traditional knowledge work inside out. Enterprises have to document not only processes but the expertise that they codify to create the automations. Organisations need to prepare for many such possibilities and adapt to ensure success. An autonomous enterprise mindset is required; start with the end in mind, focus on the 'phygital' (it's in the book, dear reader), practise good data stewardship, stay agile and be very aware of how things can go wrong. The book also rightly stresses a collaborative approach and pooling of resources. In my own research I have often found an execution gap opening up between those doing automation and those responsible for digital transformation. New silos for old. But digital transformation, to be successful, as the book makes clear, must converge digital technologies.

Enter generative AI circa November 2022. Sarah provides an easy to understand guide to what the various large language model-based systems consist of and how they operate. Like her, I am wary of the downsides that imperil the progress of these immensely powerful tools. We are early in the life cycle at the moment. Typically there are massive claims, but also much that remains unknown. There are already question marks about how much more these engines can develop. The costs of extra marginal learning may become very prohibitive, and economically not worthwhile. Part of this, as Sarah suggests, is the likely massive associated energy costs. A huge amount depends on the quality of data being drawn upon, but the dirty secret of big data is that most data being used is dirty. Statistical practices and interpretations inspire a false confidence. I am pretty sure that these systems will find their level, but by 2024/25 most organisations were struggling to work out where and how these technical developments could be applied optimally. A watching brief is a wise choice at this stage.

The book gets macro in its final chapter, being rightly less pessimistic about job losses and skills, and very clear-eyed about the ethical dimensions of using AI, and indeed all technologies. It's a book to be massively informed by, and it is clearly written, with multiple examples and well digested and analysed empirical research. Like contemporary art, only ten per cent of today's 'AI' literature is really worth engaging with. This is one of those.

Professor Leslie Willcocks
September 2024

Professor Emeritus at London School of Economics and Political Science, Associate Fellow at Green Templeton College Oxford, Research Director at Knowledge Capital Partners, and co-author of four books on automation, including Becoming Strategic with Robotic Process Automation *(SB Publishing, 2019).*

ACKNOWLEDGEMENTS

This book is the culmination of a 40-year career in IT, 10 years of which have been in the field of intelligent automation (IA), focusing on industry analysis and advisory work, with four years of specific research. During this time, I had the pleasure of working with many innovative AI and IA software developers and users, to get their perspectives on the wave of change sweeping across enterprises today, as the automation of knowledge work continues apace. There are many people who, over the years, have contributed to the knowledge that I have shared with you. I am grateful to them all. Here, I would like to thank those who have contributed most recently and specifically to this book.

Firstly, I would like to dedicate this book to my beloved late husband, Dr Tim Burnett, for the enormous support that he gave me when I was writing the first edition of this book and acting as a sounding board for my ideas. Without his boundless enthusiasm and constant encouragement, it would not have been possible.

I am grateful to all the organisations that have shared their practical perspectives with me as users of AI technology. Unfortunately I am unable to name them all except for the few who agreed to share their experiences in the named case studies provided in Part 2. I would like to thank the following for their time and the incredibly valuable and practical insights that their case studies have provided:

- Calderdale Council;
- Royal Berkshire NHS Foundation Trust;
- Siemens Global Business Services;
- Wärtsilä Marine Power.

Special thanks to Professor Leslie Willcocks for writing the foreword and patiently reviewing the interim versions of the first edition of the book. I would like to say a big thank you to Miroslaw Bartecki, Chief Technology Officer and Co-Founder at KYP.ai for reviewing the new Chapter 3 on Generative AI, and Pascal Bornet, Dr Adam Bujak, Robert Hughes and Professor Mary Lacity for reviewing the advanced original draft of the book and for the feedback that they provided.

As part of the research for this book, I interviewed a number of AI-in-business experts, users, practitioners, analysts and advisors. I am indebted to them for sharing their perspectives and views of how the market is going and evolving. My thanks to:

- Adam Bujak, CEO and Co-Founder, KYP.ai;

- Akeel Attar, CEO and Co-Founder, XpertRule;
- Alex Bentley, ex-Chief Revenue Officer, XpertRule;
- Bill Thomas, Co-Founder and ex-Chairman, Emergence Partners;
- Darrien Bold, ex-National Digital Lead for Stroke, NHS England and NHS Improvement;
- David Poole, CEO and Co-Founder, Emergence Partners – Cognition;
- Eric Simonson, Managing Partner, Everest Group;
- Francis Carden, CEO, Founder, Automation Den;
- Fred Laluyaux, CEO, Aera Technology;
- Dr George Harston, Chief Medical and Innovation Officer, Brainomix;
- Gerry Brown, CX Research Director, IDC Europe (retired);
- Dr Hannah Dee, Senior Lecturer in Computer Science, Aberystwyth University, a computer vision specialist and co-author of *Women in Tech*;
- Harri Lemmelä, Development Manager, Customer Applications, Wärtsilä Marine Power;
- John O'Connell, Director of Strategic and Service Innovation and Transformation Director, Data Analytics and Artificial Intelligence, NHS South, Central and West;
- Dr K. Nagaratnam, Consultant Stroke Physician and Geriatrician Clinical Lead for Stroke Medicine, Clinical Lead (Acute), Royal Berkshire NHSFT and ISDN Buckinghamshire, Oxfordshire and Berkshire;
- Laetitia Cailleteau, Responsible AI and Generative AI Studios Europe lead, Accenture;
- Martha Bennett, Vice President and Principal Analyst, Forrester;
- Dr Michalis Papadakis, CEO and Co-Founder, Brainomix;
- Miroslaw Bartecki, Chief Technology Officer and Co-Founder at KYP.ai
- Nikolas Barth, Global Head of Digital Transformation & Strategy and Regional Head of Digital Solutions Americas, Global Business Services, Siemens AG;
- Nuno Miguel Rocha, Digital Product Manager at Global Business Services, Siemens AG;
- Pascal Bornet, author of *Intelligent Automation*;
- Riaz Rahman, VP Healthcare Global, Brainomix;
- Richard Boyd, Principal Consultant, XpertRule;
- Robert Hughes, technology marketing executive and consultant;
- Toni Kershaw, Customer Access Manager, Calderdale Council;
- Wayne Butterfield, Partner at ISG – Global Lead, Contact Center Transformation.

PREFACE

I wrote this book simply because I had a lot to say about artificial intelligence (AI), its role in business and the road that organisations are taking towards becoming autonomous enterprises. I believe it is crucial to consider the direction this development is taking us, to understand the nature of the changes already under way, and to recognise both the opportunities we are gaining and the risks we are facing. It is by seeing the bigger picture that we can make better decisions, whether to take small, measured risks or embrace change in a 'Big Bang' approach and become more innovative and efficient in what we do.

My prediction in the first edition of this book, that enterprises will be run in a more or less autonomous way in the future, got a boost when in November 2022 OpenAI released ChatGPT-3.5 to the public for free. This is generative AI based on GPT-3.5 large language model (LLM), that has been trained on publicly available knowledge in the world up to January 2022 and other datasets. It can answer questions on a wide range of topics, generate text, poetry, write software code and do more in combination with other AI models, e.g. generate images. The release of ChatGPT-3.5 started something of an arms race among AI vendors who have followed it with their own equivalent solutions with more advanced versions coming to market in quick succession ever since, faster than most of us can keep up with. As for us users of the technology, we have since been learning how to make the most of generative AI and learning its strengths and limitations.

While I have a lot to say, I do not wish to blind readers with the science of AI. Accordingly, I have provided a high-level introduction only to deep learning because I consider it to be the most relevant to enterprise process automation. I have also provided an overview of the most prevalent enterprise-grade intelligent automation technologies. These are covered in Chapters 2 and 5 respectively. For this edition I have added the new Chapter 3 on Generative AI. I hope the information in these chapters provides you, first, with enough clarity to make sense of the content of the book and, second, with a grounding on the art of possible with AI in business to help you surf the tide of change that is sweeping the enterprise world.

Importantly, I want to emphasise the fact that you can take advantage of AI to speed your journey of change without needing to become an expert in the science of it, because computer scientists and big and small technology vendors are already doing the work for you.

AI has applications in many different fields, and it would be impossible to cover it all in one book. I have focused mine on the work that people do in corporate offices, which is commonly known as knowledge work, and is undertaken as part of their daily business processes. I have focused on knowledge work because it is changing fast and its automation will be the bedrock of autonomous enterprises of the future.

I apologise in advance for the use of a lot of IT industry and corporate jargon. Should you need it, there is a list of abbreviations complemented with a glossary of terms in the back of this book.

It has been a pleasure to write this book, part of which entailed conducting a host of interviews with experienced practitioners on how they deployed AI in their organisations. I connected to many knowledgeable and thoughtful industry experts and pundits to share our perspectives. I can honestly say that the research has enriched my knowledge and has made me hungrier for more. If I can impart a fraction of this enthusiasm to you by sharing my thoughts in this book, then I will have succeeded.

PART 1
THE RISE OF THE AUTONOMOUS ENTERPRISE

The autonomous enterprise has been in the making for centuries with every human-led technological development and advancement contributing to it. In this part of the book I describe the concept of the autonomous enterprise and the role that artificial intelligence (AI) plays in its creation. Firstly, I explain the whys and wherefores of using AI in business. These include the drivers for and the patterns of its adoption by enterprises. I provide an overview of the most dominant technological approaches to AI and its potential for innovation and efficiency. Importantly, I define the key concept of the autonomous enterprise powered by AI, and cover the technologies that are making it possible.

1   INTRODUCTION AND OVERVIEW

The ever-increasing automation of knowledge work combined with transactional process automation are leading to what I call the autonomous enterprise. In this chapter I introduce this concept and explain how artificial intelligence (AI) is making it a reality.

I explore how AI powers innovation that in turn leads to new models of business that are largely automated. I examine the business imperative that is efficiency and how this is driving business process automation and, in turn, how that is leading organisations along the road to autonomy. Furthermore, I look at the patterns of adoption of AI by enterprises.

WHAT AI AND AUTOMATION IN BUSINESS MEAN AND WHY WE NEED TO LEARN ABOUT THEM

A few decades ago it was impossible to imagine that car manufacturing processes would be almost entirely automated, with people supervising robots and control systems. Yet, this is exactly how things are done today and have been for a while too. Over the years, this high level of automation of manufacturing processes from manual to mechanised and robotised has been emulated and adopted by other industries, for example logistics and warehousing, travel and agriculture. Today it is starting to happen in an altogether different part of businesses, and that is autonomous knowledge work, the kind of work that people do in offices using their computers, and that requires know-how and both objective and subjective decision-making.

Two major forces are driving enterprises towards more autonomy in the sense of process automation: efficiency and innovation. Pressures of a competitive market keep organisations searching for more output per unit cost, and many AI-powered solutions support this objective. Similarly AI is powering the drive for innovation as large and small companies disrupt the market by bringing out novel products and services. The rush for innovation is fuelled by money pouring into the sector from investors and governments.

These two realities are coming together and leading to rapid technical advances. However, it is clear that adoption of AI is being led by large technology platform companies and start-ups. Yet, there is still plenty of potential for organisations of any type, as I explain later in this chapter and throughout the book, to tap AI to innovate and become more competitive.

This increasing level of automation of knowledge work combined with other transactional process automation is leading to what I call the autonomous enterprise, which I define in this chapter and explore extensively in Chapter 10.

In this book I focus on automation of knowledge work, but we are moving beyond the rush to digitalise these types of processes, combining them with automation in the physical world. This combination of physical and digital is sometimes referred to as 'phygital'. I address some aspects of phygital in this book as well.

Knowledge work varies from basic transactional data entry and skills-based manipulation of the data, to capturing information via interactions with others by reading documents, emails, texts and messages, looking at images or talking to people on the phone and chatting on the web. Through these interactions, knowledge workers capture information, make some form of assessment and do the necessary work or advise others based on the information and their skills and decisions. Automation of this kind of work using software with AI is still in its early phases of development and adoption. Today, it is typically applied to simpler processes where the decisions to be made are not very complex, for example does the purchase order (PO) in this invoice match our records and is the amount correct? The main difference from past office work automation is the evolving ability of machines to read and digest unstructured data, that is, information that you typically get in documents, including images and pictures, and from voice, speech and sounds.

This is in contrast to our ability to automate processes that use structured data – data that are already put into structures in a database that non-intelligent software can work with easily. Processes using structured data form the bulk of business transactions – something that we have been able to automate one way or another for decades using computer software such as accounting software or spreadsheets, that help us with complex calculations and data analysis, or customer relationship management (CRM) software that helps us manage customer information, contact details, past interactions, purchase histories and so on.

Today, we are able to automate processes that handle unstructured data thanks to intelligent software. These solutions can capture information from the unstructured data and use it to make simple decisions, for example whether to approve an invoice for payment and to activate the payment process.

The more basic and earlier approaches to automating processes that use unstructured data have involved optical character recognition (OCR). Intelligent document processing (IDP) provides a more powerful alternative to OCR. The more basic IDP, after scanning, digitises the content of paper-based documents and allows some level of automated processing of the content. Documents that can be processed with more basic capabilities are usually highly structured in templates that the software can handle. With advances in technology we can automate a lot more today, with machines able to recognise important pieces of information in unstructured documents as well as the context and the sentiment based on the use of words in the document. Methods of capturing the information have also moved well beyond OCR, from barcodes to QR codes, image and shape recognition and voice processing. The ability of machines to interact with the physical world and capture unstructured data from it has come a long way.

In voice processing for example, today, there are advanced solutions that can understand not only speech in the business context but also ordinary human utterances, as well as detecting sentiment in the tone of voice during telephone calls.

It is not just advancements in the way that we can take unstructured data into our computer systems that is allowing us to take advantage of AI, but the development of many technology ecosystems that support it. An overview of some of the most prominent ecosystems and toolkits that have made AI accessible and available for use by organisations is provided in Chapter 2.

When you combine knowledge work automation with that of other office processes, for example the kind of transactional data processing that enterprise software systems have enabled us to do for years, such as using accounting or procurement software, then companies can automate processes of low complexity from end to end. Over time with more advances in AI-enabled software we will be able to automate progressively more complex knowledge-based processes, and many of them end to end. By doing so we will achieve a significant step change in efficiency. For example, you can already have a virtual agent reply to a customer on a chat channel online and assess the tone of the conversation to determine if there is a risk of customer attrition, then make a decision about offering them a discount on the price of a product, all automatically.

Automation, when done well, increases efficiency with higher levels of straight through processing, faster response times, reduced data errors, elimination of duplicated effort, and making up for any shortages of staff and skills. These in turn lead to business outcomes such as lowered costs and higher profitability, increased capacity to take on more work to grow the business, and higher levels of customer satisfaction and brand loyalty. Existing examples include companies reporting between 83 and 196 per cent return on intelligent automation investment, adding capacity of between 168 and 697 full-time equivalent (FTE) employees over pre-automation figures, and achieving topline growth (Everest Group, 2022). These figures were provided by Everest Group, a leading industry research firm with a respected team of analysts specialising in the field of intelligent automation.

With increased automation of knowledge work, enterprises can also capture more data systematically from their enterprise software, and be able to use AI to analyse the data quickly for operational and business insights. AI can be used to join the dots to reveal hidden patterns that spell issues such as operational bottlenecks, fraudulent claims, poor performance, lack of regulatory compliance, supply chain problems and more. Taking better management of supplies as an example, as far back as 2019 Ocado was reporting benefits from AI. The UK online grocer reported that it conducted millions of demand forecasts a day using machine learning algorithms (Blake, 2022) to ensure quantity and freshness of its stock to minimise food waste. Factors considered in the forecasting include differing demand levels across markets and geographies.

Ocado also takes advantage of AI for efficiency by maintaining a digital twin – a virtual model of operations – to simulate its processes (Slegers, 2022), which allows it to optimise them end to end. In its 2019 annual report (Ocado Group, 2019) Ocado stated that, thanks to further technological improvements to its end-to-end operational capabilities across demand forecasting, inventory management and fulfilment, it had halved its food supply waste from 0.8 per cent to just 0.4 per cent of its sales. This is a double saving of costs, and food that did not end up in the waste bin.

Similar AI-powered analysis and forecasting can help organisations to spot opportunities for optimising processes, and improving or designing new products and services, therefore boosting their ability to innovate and gain a competitive edge. With innovation they can be the ones that disrupt the market rather than be disrupted by others.

AI in the form of analytics, and with its ability to spot patterns, can help enterprises even before their processes are automated. For example, there is one group of software solutions that analyse human, machine and process interactions for operational insights, to identify problems such as process bottlenecks, variations in processes that are supposed to be highly standardised and other issues such as painfully slow systems that hamper employee productivity. A lack of standardisation spells complexity and cost. Minimising variations in how processes are done by different people and parts of the organisation directly benefits the business bottom line. In some cases the process intelligence gleaned by these types of software solutions shows huge deviations from best practice and regulatory compliance as well. In these cases, the intelligent software is not only identifying where processes could be improved but helping the organisations to reduce risks, for instance, of incurring hefty regulatory fines and damage to their reputation.

THE BIRTH OF THE AUTONOMOUS ENTERPRISE

With intelligent technology enabling us to boost efficiency and innovation and minimising risks, the case for AI in business grows, and consequently, over time, we will see increased adoption. More and more of the high-volume, repetitive transactions that make up the core functions of the enterprise will be automated, just like manufacturing processes did several decades ago. This will give rise to the autonomous enterprise. This is an enterprise that:

- Conducts its core daily business functions in a digital and automated manner with minimum human touchpoints, with AI embedded in many of its systems.
- Employs people that do fewer repetitive tasks, such as checking and settling invoices, and more complex and strategic work, such as handling sensitive and complicated customer cases.
- Not only automates major operations, but empowers staff to automate their own repetitive tasks as well. The autonomous enterprise provides intelligent automation (IA) and augmentation technologies to its staff to help them work more efficiently and productively. It also offers training and support to ensure that they can use those technologies effectively.

- Takes advantage of operational data to create digital twins – virtual models of some of its critical processes – to ensure that work flows through the organisation efficiently and that there are data available to support both automated and human decision-making.

- Gathers process data that it can analyse, so that the autonomous enterprise can learn to improve operations, making it an agile and adaptive enterprise.

- Analyses data not only to make better operational decisions and to adapt to change, but also to provide support for strategic decisions, to manage the business better and, very importantly, to innovate.

The transactional work that machines do within an autonomous enterprise includes data entry, checking huge numbers of documents for information, cross-referencing and checking data for accuracy, and answering simple and repetitive enquiries at any helpdesk or in customer interactions. As more advanced intelligent systems become available, we will see the embedded AI in those systems analyse what is needed in order to do things better. Then autonomously make improvements and enhancements to processes. This is likely with developments in the field of agentic AI that is mentioned in Chapter 3: Generative AI.

The higher-value work that people do in an autonomous enterprise includes designing, implementing, overseeing, checking, maintaining and improving the AI-powered solutions that are deployed in the enterprise. Humans will also continue to oversee the automated business processes, handle cases or enquiries that are too complex for the AI to complete, plan and implement routines for the AI to capture intelligence from daily automated operations, and then, from the analysis of the intelligence, find opportunities for improving services and products to increase revenue. Accordingly, they will design new products and services, plan business growth and geographic expansion and take care of customer, supplier and partner relationships.

Organisations that have successfully integrated their data across multiple systems can go further by feeding their advanced analytics solutions, sometimes referred to as cognitive systems, with the data. This will allow the solutions to come up with answers to questions fast to guide decision-making on the fly and even have AI recommend actions, identify more opportunities for automation or activate automated procedures based on live operational indicators. Some of this is already possible with customised large language models (LLMs) that are discussed in Chapter 3: Generative AI.

The tools that empower the employees in the autonomous enterprise include AI operating as digital personal assistants that take dictation and, in more advanced cases, arrange meetings and book conference rooms or calls on behalf of the worker. The software will provide employees with collaboration insights, for example, find and connect them with colleagues who have the right expertise to be consulted when handling complex cases. The recommendations will be data-driven, based on their colleagues' past interactions and the context of their work.

Various types of digital personal assistants already exist and can provide best answers to queries based on historical information – answers provided in the past to similar questions by other employees. They can also find and guide employees to documents that show how similar requirements have been dealt with by the organisation before.

Other examples of employee tools include predictive text in email, voice-activated commands on personal productivity software, and briefings from virtual assistants on personal computers that on a daily basis remind us of commitments and follow-ups to be done and prompt us to book focus time in our diaries. This is not automation but assistance and augmentation of human work, helping people to become more productive and better at what they do.

There are already very successful examples of autonomous enterprises in existence today. Many online retailers such as Amazon and Ocado have highly automated their core functions such as sales, order fulfilment and stock controls.

Ocado conducts its business through a web-based shopfront powered by an online catalogue of products. Much of its order processing and customer interactions are digitalised. It is the same story in the order fulfilment function, which is automated with Ocado robots picking items from stocks and packing the customers' orders to be dispatched. Although many of its daily business operations are automated, there are many people at work at the company too. Behind the scenes, humans are busy building new capabilities for the company, creating new features for its website, and carrying out supply chain and order fulfilment functions. They are building partnerships, and developing new capabilities to enhance operations and more.

As a result of its digital and automated approach to selling groceries, Ocado has been able to grow and capture a strong share of the crowded UK online grocery market, estimated at 12.7 per cent according to Ocado's 2023 annual report (Ocado Group, 2023). It has been able to develop its technology and take advantage of it in multiple deals, as part of which it provides online grocery services for other major supermarkets. It is also expanding beyond the shores of the UK and building an international presence.

As another example, there is a new breed of financial services company that challenges large and established players through the use of innovative intelligent technologies. These challenger banks and insurance companies run highly automated operations using AI that speed up customer onboarding as well as other business processes: for example, know your customer (KYC) identity checks, which financial institutions are required to do for account openings, loan approvals, administration and servicing, or fully automated insurance quote, claims assessment and settlement processes.

Many people are afraid of this level of automation and in particular of the threat of job losses. That is understandable; after all, with technology to automate the work that humans have always done, what will be left for humans to do? Are humans destined to a life of unemployment misery? This is unlikely. Automation of daily business functions should not spell the end of work for humans but a change in the way that we conduct work and the nature of it. Gone will be jobs involving very repetitive and high-volume tasks such as data entry. Instead humans will be required to design, implement, manage, oversee and maintain automated processes and manage the technologies that power them. There will also be more creative roles, for example designers of customer journeys through the autonomous enterprise, to ensure the quality of service and great customer experiences. While AI may be able to help with the design of the experiences, it will need the human touch to ensure they tick all the right human-centric boxes. As for the employees of the organisations, the autonomous enterprise will enable them not only to do more interesting work but to do it better and faster – this is where human worker augmentation is already making a difference.

There are other factors too that will mean humans will continue to have work, for example the existing shortage of skills in many industries, and ageing populations in a lot of countries with low birth rates. Consequently, change is already on its way, firstly, with more technology-oriented jobs across all sectors. Secondly, demand for people in other sectors is increasing, for instance, the creative, hospitality and care sectors, and consequently making up for some of the losses in other sectors due to automation. Eurostat, the statistical office of the European Union (EU), reports that 'Service and sales workers represented the occupation with the largest share of recent job starters (24 per cent) in the third quarter of 2021' (Eurostat, 2022). Eurostat describes 'recent job starters' as recently employed, having started their job in the three months prior to the survey interview. The findings may well be simply the bounce back from lockdowns during the pandemic but there are other trends at work too. In the hospitality and entertainment sectors, for example, demand is increasing for more variety of experiences, including virtual reality and services offered digitally to people at home, for food and beverage deliveries, as well as increased hygiene requirements and safeguarding in venues. I believe these are all contributing to the trend reported by Eurostat. More on this topic follows in Chapter 11.

In the rest of the book, I focus mainly on two things that AI in business enables, and these are increased opportunities for innovation and efficiency through automation.

In recent decades, technology-powered innovation has led to a wave of companies that disrupt whole industries with new products and services or revolutionary operating models that rapidly gain market share and leave established players behind. Examples include OpenAI, Tesla, Netflix, Uber and Airbnb. The success of these companies has led to a flood of ambitious entrepreneurs wanting to emulate their success by setting up their own technology start-ups. There is a growing industry too of investors whose business is to spot the next tech-led disrupter to invest in. Subsequently, money has been pouring into AI start-ups. Generative AI is currently getting a lot of investor attention. According to S&P Global, announced generative AI investments by private equity firms reached $2.18 billion in 2023. That is more than twice the $1 billion that was invested in 2022. S&P also reported that investments in the first 2 months of 2024 alone exceeded those done in total in the first quarter of 2023 (Thomas et al., 2024). Investment in AI has been high for many years. According to research by CSET, part of Georgetown University (Arnold et al., 2020), in 2019, $40 billion was invested in AI companies by a mix of organisations from venture capital and private equity firms through to enterprises that engaged in mergers and acquisitions. These were disclosed investments that numbered 3,100 in separate transactions. There would have been many more that were not disclosed.

Governments are getting in on the act too as they strive to make their countries the next leading technology nation in the world. Across the globe, governments are implementing ambitious plans to fund technology, and in particular AI-powered start-ups, to generate wealth and jobs for their citizens. For example, the EU *White Paper* on *Artificial Intelligence: A European Approach to Excellence and Trust*, published in 2020 (European Union, 2020), sets out its ambitions to attract more than €20 billion of investment in AI each year for the next decade. The paper also highlights that in the previous three years, EU funding for research and innovation for AI rose by 70 per cent to €1.5 billion but that it lagged investments in AI in North America at €12.1 billion and in Asia at €6.5 billion. According to a paper by the European Court of Auditors titled *EU Artificial Intelligence Ambition* dated 2024, the EU's targets for private and public investment in AI were €20 billion in total from 2018 to 2020. The target today stands at €20 billion per year through to 2030 (European Court of Auditors, 2024) In May 2019 the UK Government announced its AI sector deal to harness AI and big data as one of the great opportunities of our age (UK Government, 2019). The deal was to provide a package of nearly £1 billion of support for the sector, with contributions from the government, industry and academia, with £603 million in newly allocated funding and up to £342 million from existing budgets, alongside £250 million for connected and autonomous vehicles. More plans are sure to follow with a new government that got into office in July 2024.

With investment pouring into the sector, more innovation and disruption are certain to happen, and no organisation can afford to be left behind. This is why I cover innovation both in this chapter and in more detail in Chapter 4: AI for Innovation.

Business efficiency has been a priority for every boardroom since the beginning of commerce with enterprises taking all kinds of measures to achieve it. I will recap some of these measures and how AI can change them later in this chapter and in more detail in Chapter 5: AI for Efficiency.

AI FOR INNOVATION

I came across a good example of innovative uses of AI a few years ago when I visited a healthcare company in San Francisco. Although a start-up, its healthcare app had already been adopted by various business customers around the world. The healthcare app ran on mobile phones and remotely connected doctors to patients for health advice and consultation via video calls. This was innovative at the time but it wasn't the only feature of the technology-enabled service. The app also used AI to check the patients' symptoms and to connect them to doctors with a track record of dealing with similar conditions or illnesses. The AI conversed with the patient and used their symptoms and health records to determine the probable cause of the problem before referring them to a doctor. Additionally, it pooled advice that had been provided previously by doctors for similar conditions to provide information to the patient. The app had already been adopted by a healthcare insurance firm to provide improved and differentiated services to its clients, and the start-up had more prospects on the horizon.

On another occasion, I visited a large German manufacturer to see its use of AI in manufacturing process simulation, visualisation and digital twins (in this case a digital version of the human worker at their workstation). These provided information on how to optimise the manufacturing processes as well as the ergonomics of the human workstation on assembly lines. The more its processes were optimised the faster it could manufacture its products as well as keep its staff happy and comfortable during their shifts.

Another time, in an innovation centre in Silicon Valley, I saw a futuristic demonstration of AI in eLearning in 3D using holographic imagery that would guide field engineers to fix broken machinery at customer sites. This type of solution has good potential for field operations, including maintenance of vending machines and repair of home appliances.

Recently, generative AI has shown us that computers can generate code (e.g. develop a whole new website) based on human instructions. Even as far back as 2019 there were developments with automated code generation. Back then, I learnt about an IA vendor working on a new feature to partially automate the coding of robots in its robotic process automation (RPA) software, using task mining and AI. This aimed to speed up process automation and consequently improve the return on investment (RoI) in the technology. Firstly, the task of identifying candidate processes for automating with RPA was accelerated using the task mining component of the software. Secondly, the codification of the identified process was made faster using the semi-automated intelligent robot code generation that created the template for the task. This remains an exciting development for me because a few years prior to that I had predicted that RPA software would enable the automation of automations – robots generating the software code for new robots (Burnett, 2019). The technologists among you will be familiar with low- and no-code development environments. The idea of this solution took the concept further by first discovering what process could be automated and then helping with the automatic automation of that process. Today, this is possible with generative AI in many different settings, for example web design and development, and plain and simple software development.

These are very different examples of uses of AI but, in all the cases, the companies have grabbed the opportunity offered by AI to develop innovative solutions. The history of business is strewn with examples of innovations that have disrupted industries and transformed one or more aspects of work or social models, for example cloud computing, social media and companies that have disrupted whole industries such as Uber and Airbnb. For every company that advances thanks to its innovation, there are many that fail to change with some ending up in corporate graveyards.

Enterprises cannot afford to fall behind in AI-powered innovation because there are market forces that are driving it and billions of pounds of private equity and other money pouring into the sector, as discussed previously.

AI is a particularly good enabler of innovation because, firstly, it allows us to automate things that we couldn't have done before, for example reading unstructured documents and humans conversing with machines in natural languages. Secondly, it brings us insights through advanced analytics, fast.

> I was involved in an AI learning project a while ago. The exercise was to write code to test the likelihood of a banking customer registering for a new service. The analysis took into account various factors such as the customer's income and past history. We used Python and a neural network provided by Keras (Keras, n.d.), an open library that works on top of TensorFlow, using a large anonymised dataset. In this basic learning exercise, we were able to get accuracy of prediction of over

11

92 per cent. The whole thing took us 1½ days, spread over a number of days, and that included debugging the code. This type of operational analytics would have required new ways of thinking if we were using more traditional statistical analysis tools. The actual analysis, the algorithm running through the data, would have taken a long time as well without a neural network. The potential of this type of rapid operational analysis is huge, and I encourage you to think of the possibilities for your organisation.

Keras is just one of many libraries that are available to the world to learn and practise AI for real. Chapter 2 provides an introduction to some of these types of resources as well as the science of neural networks, a key enabler of AI.

AI FOR EFFICIENCY

In the context of this book, efficiency is the effectiveness with which a company conducts its business. It is the amount of work that it does and the costs that it incurs compared to the results that it achieves. It is a simple maths equation, and if the balance tilts too much towards expenses and work and energy expended, then costs accumulate and profits decline. If this type of scenario continues and no action is taken to address it, a downward spiral begins that could result in the company going out of business.

Efficiency is something that organisations have strived for since the dawn of commerce. Here is a quick recap of the measures most frequently used in the late 20th and 21st centuries:

- **Methodologies such as Lean, Six Sigma and Agile**: Lean and Six Sigma were extremely popular approaches for process and business optimisation for decades. More recently Agile has been adopted for business management but its roots are steeped in best practice for software projects. Software solutions for business process management and optimisation are increasingly being used as well.

- **Centralisation and shared services centres (SSCs) concepts and practice**: shared services took the concept of specialist bureaus that emerged in the 1950s further to deliver dedicated, expert, standardised and quality services to a group of business units within large companies, for example finance and accounting services, human resources (HR) or customer contact services. In this model, the parent companies transfer the need for business function and process efficiency to the centre managers. Often, they make them responsible for their centre's commercial viability and increasing year-on-year efficiency. The managers, in turn, invest in skills, systems and process standardisation to ensure continuous improvement to meet their performance targets. That said, after years of year-on-year improvements, many SSC managers say that they run out of options to achieve yet more demanding efficiency targets set by their parent companies. This is why they welcome developments in technology that allow them to do more for less.

- **Labour arbitrage, off-shoring and near-shoring**: the location of shared services became an important aspect of cost efficiency as well with shared services centres being placed in countries where the cost of staffing them was lower than Western

Europe or North America. Later, the model evolved further with more specialist services being placed closer to home, for example in Eastern Europe for Western European businesses, or South America for North American companies. Today, companies use a mix of off-shore, near-shore and on-shore (in the home country) shared services centres to optimise the model according to the specialisation of each centre. For example, you might have general accounting and transactional finance services off-shore, the management of the finance software near-shore and strategic management on-shore. The labour arbitrage equation is getting diluted with salaries going up because of a shortage of skills in many popular off-shore and near-shore delivery locations. Another challenge in off-shore locations is the relatively high price of software licences when currency exchange rates are taken into account. The cost can become a barrier to investment.

- **Outsourcing**: this is another approach to the continued search for business efficiency. In outsourcing, a whole function or a group of business services are outsourced to specialist outsourcing companies, who deliver them either as a specific or as part of a shared services model from off-, near- or on-shore locations, using either their own software platforms, for example banking systems for banking clients, or the client's own systems, which they access remotely. Outsourcing companies continually invest in technology, methodologies and skills in order to offer specialist services at attractive prices. They also offer different models of services such as dedicated and pooled, with options and different pricing levels that include contributing to the modernisation of a service, gainshare and outcome-based pricing. More automation in their clients' enterprises, however, will no doubt impact their business models.

- **Digitalisation of services**: investing in new systems, typically cloud-native solutions that run on cloud infrastructure, has been a key pillar of transforming and modernising the corporate technology landscape. This reduces the upfront costs of investment and turns capital expense (CapEx) into operational expense (OpEx) that can be absorbed by the business throughout the year. Digitalisation also supports the pivot to online services with virtual self-service becoming the standard way of interacting with customers. Self-service is an incredibly efficient way of providing customers with information about products and services as well as allowing them to choose and customise what they want and order it all from the comfort of their computers. The model provides fast and complete virtualisation of services with, ideally, the only customer contact being at the point of delivery.

Of course, digitalisation can result in reduced social and business contact for people and cause problems for those who do not have access to technology. Many businesses continue to offer alternative channels of interactions, for example banks offering phone and branch-based banking, but governments need to act to ensure that those channels do not disappear completely over time.

Each lever mentioned above is capable of generating efficiency savings to some degree, and when combined together, as is often practised by businesses, significant benefits can be achieved. Add AI-enabled capabilities and the outcomes can be considerably boosted. The term 'a step change' is used too often in the context of business process efficiency, but there is evidence to show that it is true when AI is involved. In 2020 and 2022 Everest Group (2020, 2022) assessed multiple enterprises for the maturity of their adoption of IA solutions. Participants included Siemens Global Business Services, which is the subject of a case study in Chapter 6.

> Intelligent automation (IA) is a term that refers to solutions that use some forms of AI to automate business processes. They include RPA with computer vision and intelligent management of robots, intelligent document processing (IDP) and chatbots.

In the first of its reports, published in 2020, Everest Group identified 8 of the 49 companies that it assessed as Pinnacle Enterprises™. These had outperformed the rest of the group in terms of the sophistication and maturity of their adoption of IA and the results that they had achieved. The research found that: 50 per cent of the Pinnacle Enterprises had achieved cost savings of more than 60 per cent in the process area where IA had been applied; the other 50 per cent reported savings of between 20 per cent and 60 per cent in the same context. Also, out of the remaining group of 41 companies, 29 per cent had achieved cost savings of over 60 per cent, and 44 per cent had achieved cost savings of between 20 per cent and 60 per cent.

The results are highlighted in Figure 1.1.

Figure 1.1 Impact of IA initiatives on costs, percentage of respondents (Source: Everest Group, 2020)

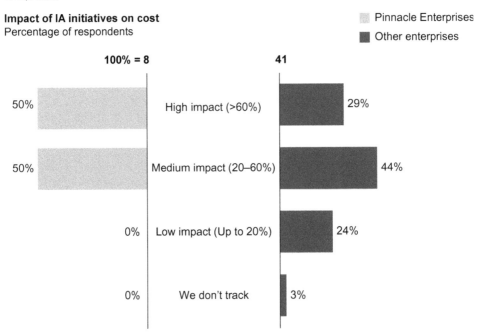

Impact of IA initiatives on cost
Percentage of respondents

Pinnacle Enterprises
Other enterprises

100% = 8   41

50%	High impact (>60%)	29%
50%	Medium impact (20–60%)	44%
0%	Low impact (Up to 20%)	24%
0%	We don't track	3%

AI was one of the major factors that separated the eight top performers, the Pinnacle Enterprises, from the rest of the group of companies:

- A total of 75 per cent of the Pinnacle Enterprises had deployed machine learning for document classification and data extraction.
- A total of 63 per cent had also deployed intelligent capabilities for computers to process documents and natural language, known as natural language processing (NLP) and text analytics.
- The remaining 41 enterprises showed far lower adoption of AI, with only 38 per cent having adopted machine learning for document classification and data extraction.
- Only 22 per cent of the rest had adopted more advanced NLP and text analytics.

These results are shown in Figure 1.2.

Figure 1.2 Sophistication level of OCR/IDP deployed, percentage of respondents
(Source: Everest Group, 2020)

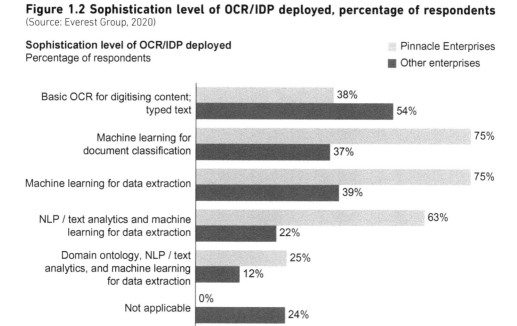

In its second report, published in 2022, Everest Group identified 10 of 55 enterprises as Pinnacle Enterprises. The participants reported much higher benefits from their investment in IA technologies compared to those that took part in the first report. Improvements included faster breaking even with the costs of investments in IA, better returns on investments, and higher levels of operational and business impact achieved. These are summarised in Figure 1.3.

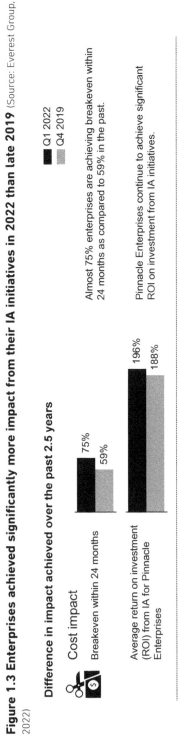

Figure 1.3 Enterprises achieved significantly more impact from their IA initiatives in 2022 than late 2019 (Source: Everest Group, 2022)

Difference in impact achieved over the past 2.5 years

Q1 2022
Q4 2019

Cost impact

Breakeven within 24 months — 75% / 59%

Almost 75% enterprises are achieving breakeven within 24 months as compared to 59% in the past.

Average return on investment (ROI) from IA for Pinnacle Enterprises — 196% / 188%

Pinnacle Enterprises continue to achieve significant ROI on investment from IA initiatives.

Operational impact

Improvement in turnaround time for Pinnacle Enterprises — 70% / 57%

Improvement over pre-intelligent automation in turnaround time is 70% as compared to 57%, 2.5 years ago.

Business impact

Improvement in top-line growth of Pinnacle Enterprises — 63% / 33%

Enterprises are realising high impact in strategic areas. Improvement in top-line growth of Pinnacle Enterprises™ has increased by almost 2× over 2.5 years ago.

A number of factors were cited as drivers of better outcomes since the first Everest Group Pinnacle study was published in 2020. These included larger scale, wider scope and speed of adoption of IA technologies, helped by better skills that inevitably come with experience of implementing technology. Another factor was a data-driven approach to choosing what to automate, thanks to the enterprises' use of process and task mining tools that provided actionable operational intelligence.

While all of the phenomenal savings achieved by the Pinnacle Enterprises in the Everest Group reports cannot be attributed to AI alone, it is clear that AI can substantially lift efficiency. The other two significant contributing factors to the outcomes were optimising processes before automating them and sharing resources. The Pinnacle Enterprises had bet heavily on best practice, and this too had paid off for them. They harnessed the power of AI and machine learning technology and combined it with the rigour of their approach.

Other studies have shown that AI can deliver significant benefits. Early examples include the programme known as FUDIPO (Open Access Government, 2020) which showed that AI can reduce energy consumption when used for plant-wide monitoring and control of data-intensive processes. FUDIPO comprised a set of proofs of concepts (PoCs) conducted as part of a European Commission-funded project under the H2020 programme, SPIRE-02-2016 topic and in partnership with Mälardalen University in Sweden. It ran between 2016 and 2020. The PoCs found that the use of AI for predictive data analysis and controls resulted in energy savings in various industries including oil refineries and water treatment plants. The findings show that the application of AI in the context of monitoring and control of data-intensive processes can generate huge energy savings when applied in different industries. The preliminary results were published by Open Access Government (Open Access Government, 2020; Dahlquist, 2020) showing the following levels of annual energy savings were possible based on the FUDIPO PoCs:

- 86–95 terawatt hours per year (TWh/y) in pulp and paper processing;
- 120–200 TWh/y in oil refineries;
- 17–41 TWh/y in wastewater treatment.

These would add up to total savings of 353–526 TWh/y, equivalent to 3 per cent of all energy used within the EU for all purposes.

When AI is combined with other technologies it amplifies efficiency by enabling more of each business process to be automated than is possible when using non-intelligent software alone. This is primarily because it allows companies to automate processes that handle both transactional data (i.e. structured data) and unstructured data in documents and other types of content. It can also take data from sources such as files or devices, and analyse them to provide predictive analytics and intelligent controls. Consequently, more of each process can be automated, with straight through processing increased substantially. AI can also enhance or replace the other efficiency levers that I have described above, as shown in Table 1.1.

Table 1.1 How AI can enhance the more traditional levers that companies have used for business efficiency

Traditional lever	Examples of how AI can boost the outcomes
Methodologies such as Lean, Six Sigma and Agile	Process/task and productivity intelligence software, powered by AI, can automatically identify process optimisation opportunities at a detailed level and provide comprehensive operational and performance intelligence to allow companies to improve business functions and productivity levels. With automatic collection and integration of process data, the tools remove the need for manual work, for example when process optimisation consultants interview process experts and shadow them for hours to learn what needs improving and how. Users of productivity intelligence solutions report saving many human years' worth of manual effort by automating the information gathering part of process reviews.
Centralisation and SSCs and practice	With the potential of other more traditional levers for efficiency exhausted, SSCs are increasingly looking at intelligent solutions to achieve additional year-on-year efficiency savings. This includes use of technology to digitalise and automate processes, e.g. by increasing the use of chatbots and virtual assistants to handle incoming enquiries and adding AI-enabled next best action advice to improve productivity and response times in contact centres, information technology (IT), HR or other helpdesk functions. Additionally, task and productivity intelligent solutions are enabling data-driven pricing for services based on actual process completion data.
Labour arbitrage, off-shoring and near-shoring	Partial automation or augmentation can boost employee productivity no matter where they are located. It can free up office workers to do more interesting work as well, e.g. from doing basic data entry to being retrained to work in an automation centre of excellence or to do other more complex work such as production of management reports. IA can also change the location needs of the organisation, and increase the use of near-shore or on-shore resources while keeping costs low. This is not good news for the mass production and outsourcing service centres of the world, but they too are building their AI skills to improve the efficiency of their services to continue to offer attractive propositions to other countries. Additionally, they are expanding more and more into software and technology product development.

(Continued)

Table 1.1 (Continued)

Traditional lever	Examples of how AI can boost the outcomes
Outsourcing	Increasing levels of automation in outsourcing contracts can lead to adoption of different pricing models, changing from input or headcount-based pricing to outcome or gainshare models. More services could be brought in-house while those that remain outsourced could deliver additional benefits such as service providers being able to increase year-on-year efficiency savings thanks to the insights that they get when they automate their processes. In terms of pricing, some organisations are already using task mining and productivity intelligence as the basis of their service pricing based on actual process data, e.g. throughput.
Digitalisation of services	Digital transformation has been going on for years but it is evolving. With AI, digital can become intelligent, that is, software-based business and consumer solutions that use AI in some form or other, e.g. the healthcare app that uses AI to check the user's symptoms. The number of solutions that take advantage of AI in some form or other is increasing fast. The uses pertain not only to end-user applications but also to how companies find insights and information, how they optimise and automate their business processes, transport and logistics operations, IT maintenance and more. AI can be used to better maintain IT infrastructure and systems and improve desktop support. Another use case is automatically managing and monitoring devices and machinery thanks to AI checking their status via the Internet of Things (IoT) and analysing the data that it gathers. Even traditional businesses such as farming and agriculture are starting to adopt AI, be it in the form of intelligent weeding of crops to robots picking fruit and vegetables, or autonomous farm vehicles.

GOING FROM DIGITAL TO PHYGITAL

Levels of automation and augmentation of operations and processes in enterprises have been increasing steadily over the past two decades. Until recently, all the attention was on increasing virtual interactions and digitalisation of processes enabling customer self-service and personalisation. The COVID-19 pandemic with its lockdowns and the shift to working from home increased the take-up of digital channels, while behind the scenes, organisations invested in automation of processes to make up for staff shortages due to the pandemic. As the digitalisation of processes continues, we will increasingly need to join the digital world to the physical world. It is the combination of the two that is referred to as phygital (physical+digital). Examples include taking orders for products online and then having automated order fulfilment processes, such as robots in the warehouse, to get the physical product to the client. These are the kinds of extensively automated processes that we will see more of in the autonomous enterprises of the future. I provide many examples of phygital throughout the book and in particular in Chapter 4, where I examine the opportunities for innovation with AI.

To illustrate the concept in this chapter I focus on its application in marketing.

The marketing automation imperative in a phygital world

In the context of marketing, one challenge for enterprises that have made digital their main channel of interactions with their customers is to do better than their competitors and differentiate their online capabilities, shopfronts and apps from others. The result is a host of offerings that often bridge the divide between the physical and digital worlds. For example:

- Retailers that provide apps for improved in-store shopping experiences, for example customise and order online, then try and buy in-store with your order identified using the store app on your mobile phone.

- Offers on single tariffs for electricity at home and for electric cars combined with a smart and connected electricity meter in the home.

- Phone companies that offer tickets for entertainment and experiences that are highly in demand.

Managing such arrays of offerings requires a lot of administration and handling of data that would need to be updated across multiple systems with confirmations, notifications, alerts and information sent to the customer, as well as partners, service providers, company divisions and operational teams. These create a huge workload for every organisation that offers them. In the autonomous enterprise, these transactions would be mostly automated in a joined-up fashion.

The capture of transactional data to be analysed for insights, such as the customer's buying patterns and preferences, is not a new thing, but in the autonomous enterprise these would be powered by AI to gain better personalised services, offers and more business intelligence such as propensity to buy a new product or likelihood of applying for a new store card.

The same automated approach can be used to help with managing customer contact better; for example if changes to the customer's data are automatically propagated across systems, it ensures that they are always up to date. Consequently, should a client call the customer contact number, in the autonomous enterprise both robots and human agents will have access to the latest customer information to handle the call quickly and efficiently.

AI ADOPTION

Research that I conducted for this book between November 2020 and January 2021 showed that many organisations were still at the beginning of AI adoption. The purpose of this research was to find out which types of companies were advertising for AI skills in the UK. The study examined 200 unique non-academic AI-related job vacancies advertised on two major job sites. It found that 60 per cent of the 200 were posted by technology companies, start-ups or consultancies that needed skills either to build or enhance their own AI-powered products or to have in place for client projects. The split of job adverts by enterprises on the sell-side of the market, that is technology vendors, consultancies and service providers, versus the buy-side of the market, for instance buyers of technologies and related services, is shown in Figure 1.4.

Figure 1.4 The split of adverts for AI skills by sell-side and buy-side of the technology market based on 2020 data

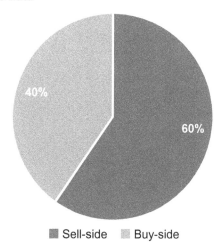

40%

60%

■ Sell-side　▦ Buy-side

Advertisers from companies that were not in the business of selling technology-based solutions or related services were in the minority, accounting for 40 per cent of the adverts. These included banks, insurance and telecommunication companies, car manufacturers, and a small number of primary healthcare providers. Many of these companies were major global businesses, some with their own technology arms, that you would expect to see on the list.

I repeated the exercise in Q1 of 2024 to find that the picture had reversed itself. More buy-side organisations were advertising vacancies for AI-related jobs than previously.

The chart is shown in Figure 1.5.

Figure 1.5 The split of adverts for AI skills by sell-side and buy-side of the technology market based on 2024 data

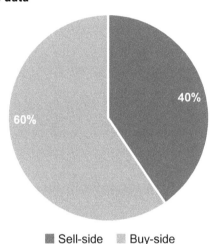

- ■ Sell-side   ▦ Buy-side

This switch between the buy-side and the sell-side of the market is a natural development in an emerging field of computing. Technology vendors and service providers recruited early in their AI product life cycle back in 2020 when I first did the research. The buy-side of the market, the users of those products, are today investing in skills in order to make the most of those offerings. The availability of generative AI must have played a role in the uptick in buy-side recruitment of AI skills. ChatGPT-3.5 has played an important role in demonstrating the scope of possibilities of AI to the world, inspiring corporate decision-makers to take advantage of the technology.

Of the 202 unique AI job adverts that were current at the time of my research in Q1 2024, 20 were in academia and were not included in the buy-side versus the sell-side data.

The picture by industry remained similar to the 2020 data in that the computer software and technology-related services industry had the most adverts but there were companies in more industries advertising than before, leading to the higher number of vacancies on the buy-side of the market in total.

The study confirms take-up of AI by enterprises, firstly by the sell-side of the market as vendors and service providers continue to cater for the growing demand for AI-powered software solutions. On the buy-side, there is hiring in order to implement the technologies that are becoming increasingly intelligent.

Figure 1.6 shows the split of job adverts for AI skills by industry based on the Q1 2024 research data

In terms of roles advertised the use of titles such as 'AI/ML engineers' has overtaken 'data scientist' in being the most in demand. Figure 1.7 shows the frequency of adverts by job type. In this context, it is important to note that there was much overlap between

Figure 1.6 Split of the AI job adverts researched in 2024, by industry

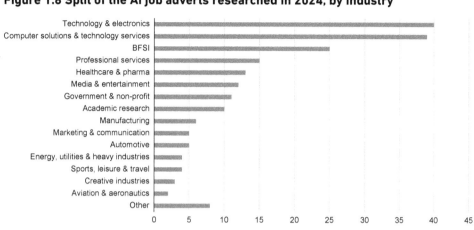

Figure 1.7 Jobs by role based on 2024 data

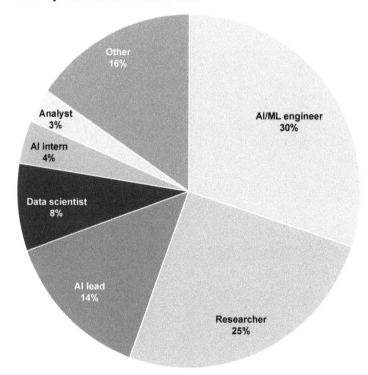

job descriptions. For example, adverts for machine learning (ML) or AI researchers often mentioned the need for the candidate to work on data science projects, and engineers needed for data science and vice versa.

Unsurprisingly, the giants of the technology industry were well represented in the sample. While we cannot necessarily emulate what these massive companies can do with their deep pockets and unlimited resources, we can follow their principles of never standing still, and investing in technology and skills in the best way that we can, to gain and keep a leading edge in our own lines of business. Investing in AI today is a must because, like it or not, it is here and is enabling modernisation and disruption at orders of magnitude bigger than any previous technology.

I cover what AI is in Chapter 2 but only to set the scene without going too deep into the science of it. My reason for this is that computer scientists are developing intelligent solutions and AI platforms for us. Businesses only need to understand the basics and to learn the art of the possible with a host of free and commercial AI resources and products out there in the software market.

SUMMARY

In this chapter I have provided a round-up of all the most important topics related to AI in business, including its ability to automate operations and, importantly, knowledge work; the journey that we are on towards the autonomous enterprise; the rise of generative AI; some focus on phygital; the power of AI to help enterprises innovate and make a step change in efficiency; the future of work for humans; and the current state of AI adoption by enterprises. I have provided information on how advances in technology are quickening and how money is pouring into the sector. I have also shown that companies from many different industries are investing in AI. This information should completely clear any doubts in the mind of decision-makers as to why they need to understand the potential of AI in business and invest in it.

In the rest of the book I delve deeper into these topics, starting with an overview of the science of AI in the next chapter.

2   WHAT YOU NEED TO KNOW ABOUT AI

Anyone's imagination would be stretched by the possibilities presented by AI today. Its current capabilities and rate of development provide the potential for new types of enterprise and service.

As you think about the innovation or efficiency initiatives that might move your organisation towards an autonomous enterprise, you need to know a few facts about AI:

- It is a disruptive technology and so you can expect your own market to change. At the end of the chapter I suggest how you can start now and lead that disruption rather than wait for others to take the initiative.

- One impact of AI is that enterprises will look at IT with a different perspective. This has happened before when many organisations found they had to reorganise to make use of the web and mobile technologies. AI will extend this need for change, and in this book I explain some of the new roles required to make the most of the more intelligent components.

- Solutions will rapidly evolve to meet common requirements. In this book, I use the loose term 'toolkits' to describe this range of solutions. They range from packaged software with the ability to configure some AI features, through to technically complex code libraries and everything in between. It is a new market so the catch-all term 'toolkit' covers all the different types of software that have emerged.

- You will probably need to build relationships with new vendors or reassess how much development you take on in-house as your AI initiatives progress. In this chapter I describe some signs of things to come and predict the types of products and vendors that will spring up.

Before going into detail about these practical considerations I provide a bit of historical background and then talk about the types of solutions that are being developed in the market. I then describe some of the underlying technology. Some readers may want to skip the more technical sections or go back to them for reference. I then circle back to the types of solutions that are available, or soon will be, and from there provide some guidance on the key decisions to be taken as you look at your organisation afresh.

THE EVOLUTION OF AI AND WHY IT IS RAPIDLY ADVANCING NOW

AI has a long history, first in the minds of theoretical mathematicians and computer scientists, then in sci-fi movies and from there into the real world. From the 1950s to the 1980s progress was relatively slow. Computers could be programmed to perform specific tasks at incredible speed. To a limited degree these programs could 'learn' and improve. Milestones such as Deep Blue's chess victory over Gary Kasparov in 1997 grabbed headlines. It then took another two decades before AlphaGo beat a professional player, Fan Hui (Williams, 2019), an event that underscored the advance into the more abstract reasoning required by the game of Go. AI was still not making a big impact on our business or domestic lives, but in the last seven to eight years the technology has permeated our everyday routines, and the pace of this is quickening.

To distil the aspects of this technology that will be useful to a business manager, I explain the new market for tools that allow AI to be applied directly to a business problem. For most enterprises and government organisations the best way to use AI is through a software tool that allows a business problem to be addressed directly. In this book, I call software products of that type a toolkit. These toolkits allow a business function to be configured in a non-technical environment by a team who understand the business problem to be addressed but who do not want to get involved in technical implementation detail. There are many toolkits and they provide functions as varied as automated document processing and hazard avoidance through to eRecruitment and conversational interfaces on enterprise resource planning (ERP) systems.

This chapter describes the types of toolkit available and then goes into some detail about the machine learning and, in particular, the deep learning technology on which many of them rely. Having delved into the underpinning technology, I go back to the types of toolkits to explain how they can best be used and the skills needed to exploit them.

BREAKING IT DOWN: MAKING AI WORK FOR YOU

The technical environment you need in order to get the benefits from AI will be influenced by many factors specific to your own organisation's history, resources and future direction. On the assumption that few will be able to establish a business case to create AI solutions from scratch, most will use one or several of the many toolkits available. The market for toolkits is relatively new and is changing fast. To put some structure on this rapidly evolving landscape, I first classify the toolkits into the type of problem they are addressing. Figure 2.1 illustrates this classification, and below I describe the layers in more detail.

The top of the diagram represents the layer that interacts with people or maybe other machines, across all the different types of toolkits: a speech interface, a conversational text-based interface or any other type of interaction.

The rest of the layers, the toolkits currently on the market that provide AI, can then be split into five major categories:

- Configurable business solutions that use AI as an embedded element.
- Business function toolkits that can present a user interface directly or are intended to be used by a higher-level business solution.
- Specific functions that can be assembled together, for example document processing requires NLP as well as aspects of image recognition.

- Foundation models that power large language models (LLMs) and other generative AI.

- Underlying technology toolkits that provide facilities for building and training deep learning systems but without needing to get down to the detail.

Figure 2.1 Overview of the types of AI toolkit

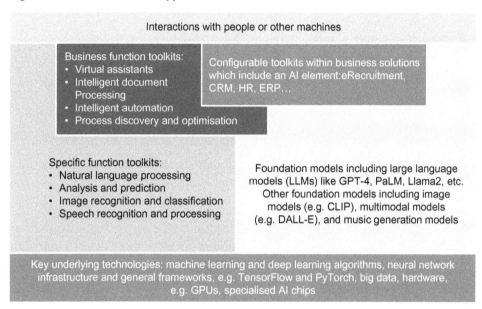

It is important to note that this is a simplified view, and the lines can be blurry and overlap. For example, some foundation models might have some built-in capabilities for NLP tasks, and configurable toolkits could tap specific function toolkits as well. Figure 2.1 is intended to help put some context around the AI terms that you might hear, what they represent and how they relate to each other.

I am going to take a look at each layer in Figure 2.1 and the types of toolkit in turn to help you select the group that meets your business need or area of interest.

Configurable toolkits within business solutions

Every major vendor of packaged applications for the enterprise market has made announcements about their current and future use of AI including generative AI. If your organisation has existing investments in these applications, then exploring their AI roadmap would be a good starting point. Some of the common features being added to solutions, depending on their functionality, include:

- conversational user interfaces;

- automated text generation, summarisation and translation;

- voice processing including conversion to text and instantaneous translation;
- image, video and music generation including text to image conversion;
- ability to automate more processes, particularly interfaces with customers and suppliers;
- better predictions from analytics modules;
- analysis of complex data provided in simple to follow natural language leading to developments such as automated advice for employees: for example next best action for call centre agents;
- automated advice for customers: such as conversational diagnostic guides and virtual customer service agents;
- devices that are automatically monitored, possibly in combination with the IoT.

The aim of each vendor is to make their solutions comprehensive enough for their market while also keeping the solutions easy to use and configure. The list is illustrative and is being expanded all the time as vendors build or acquire new functionality. The advantage of following a vendor roadmap is that the development and integration risks are handled by the supplier but it is unlikely to be the least costly approach and will always lag the state-of-the-art by a few release cycles. The lag is caused by the time required by the vendor to implement new features and complete the required compatibility testing across a broad suite of modules and also provide an acceptable upgrade path for the installed software base. Unsurprisingly, this means that single product vendors and open-source projects can usually release new functionality more quickly.

Business function toolkits

It may be that packaged applications do not allow your business to differentiate itself in the marketplace or are moving too slowly. If you determine that some aspect of your business has specific needs, then there are toolkits for many purposes and the range is expanding daily. Those on the market typically cover one of the following areas:

- IDP systems that scan and interpret forms, reports and correspondence and capture information from them.
- Intelligent virtual agents/assistants (IVAs), some of which are powered by generative AI, can provide a service to your customers or employees by guiding them through processes or answering questions about your products and services.
- Other intelligent automation, also referred to as intelligent process automation (IPA) allows organisations to start to move away from processes that are defined once and get re-engineered periodically to business flows that can continually improve.
- Process discovery and optimisation automatically capture and integrate process data to bring visibility into an organisation's operations. They map out processes and identify issues and bottlenecks. Solutions include process and task mining that are used extensively by enterprises to identify where automation makes sense in a maze of business processes.

I think the market will settle on some specific AI functions that are used across many organisations, and a new form of packaged software market will emerge. Software in this new market will draw less of a distinction between defining a function or process at 'design time' and then continuing with that process in production until it is re-engineered. Rather the software itself will guide the analyst and developer towards a solution that satisfies the business requirement, taking into account the results from real data along the way. The solution will not be static but will continue to learn.

Learning is an inherent aspect of AI, but in Chapter 4 of this book we explore the impact on a typical software development cycle. Tooling has emerged that applies AI to the design of processes as well as the execution of those processes. I believe this could make a fundamental difference to the way organisations view their software development projects, but will leave further discussion to Chapter 4.

Specific function toolkits: AI services

Continuing our journey down the layers of toolkits illustrated in Figure 2.1, it may be that you evaluate the business function toolkits that are available and decide that none of them meets your business needs, in which case there are products that allow you to more directly manage the AI. From the research that I have conducted for this book, and the case studies in it and other sources, it is clear that most of the current applications of AI in business today rest on one of the following functions:

- natural language processing;
- analysis and prediction;
- image recognition and classification;
- speech recognition.

There are many other problems that can be addressed by AI, but most of the examples in this book use toolkits that include one or more of these capabilities. Looking at the same situation from an alternative viewpoint, most toolkits that are available as a product are covered by this list.

Natural language processing
NLP is the technology that allows speech and text to be analysed and used within software systems. It is the technology used by the virtual assistant on your phone that responds to your voice commands. Language processing is now so good that many more uses have opened up, including chatbots using large language models, referred to as generative AI that is discussed extensively in Chapter 3.

You can use NLP directly in your projects by, for example, running all your customer comments for a week through a sentiment analysis tool to understand whether your service or product is improving. If you get that same feedback in the form of documents from, say, intermediaries in the supply chain, then the combination of NLP and image recognition have greatly improved the reliability of automated document handling and consequently made the analysis of feedback more comprehensive and reliable.

NLP underpins all the conversational interfaces and speech recognition technology used in the examples in this chapter. If you want to ease your organisation into AI then NLP could be a good place to start.

Data analysis and prediction

The same family of technologies that have advanced language processing can be applied to many prediction tasks. What is the likelihood of default on a credit card account? What healthcare outcome can we expect from a set of personal or population data?

As long as you have sufficient good quality data to train the AI, then you can use them to look for and identify patterns in the behaviour of your products, customers and partners. You can then predict the likelihood of key events, for example customers switching or purchasing something, or partners defecting.

One growing use of analysis, pattern recognition and prediction is in business process optimisation and exception handling. The business processes that are the lifeblood of organisations have been examined, re-engineered and changed as different management methodologies find favour, as described in Chapters 1 and 5. AI can be used to provide a new perspective.

Many automated processes are plagued by exceptions that require human intervention, for example when, due to duplicated records in a database, the identity and residential address of a person cannot be confirmed automatically, or when a chatbot cannot handle a conversation because it is beyond its training. Exceptions like these are passed to humans to handle. The people involved with these processes soon get to understand the reason for the failure of the automated process when faced with the exceptions, but can make process changes to iron out the exceptions, depending on their priorities and the availability of resources to make the changes.

AI is very good at finding patterns in unstructured data and these can be used to automate exception handling. For example, you have been running the same process in accounts payable for two years. You are finding that 10 per cent of invoices need some manual intervention before they can be receipted. You either re-engineer the processes or you can automatically classify the exception and then automate the corrective action. You can call in some consultants or you can run the historic data through a neural network and find out what led to the exceptions. Neural networks are very good at finding a way to make predictions from data but not so good at explaining why those predictions work. This is a research field that is advancing rapidly. Why were invoice mistakes more common on a Friday? What led to the discount period being missed most frequently? These exceptions can be discovered by people, but a neural network will look for patterns and, if there is one, it will find it to allow your domain experts to determine the root cause. If there is no pattern in the data, you will find that too and save a bunch on fees.

Image recognition and object detection

Image recognition is used for mainstream applications such as number plate recognition, and there are countless other applications of image and object recognition that confer significant business advantage, such as:

- recognising a spare part from a photo sent in by a customer;

- diagnosing a fault from a photograph of an appliance combined with an error code from the same image;
- damage assessment during insurance claim processing;
- enhancing business processes and models if the image or object recognition is sufficiently reliable.

Huge improvements in image classification systems were highlighted by the renowned ImageNet Large Scale Visual Recognition Challenge. From 2010 to 2017 the performance of the contender systems continually improved and overtook the ability of humans in this space. Specific milestones came with the use of convolutional neural networks. With developments in this field, the commercially available toolkits get close to the performance seen in these competitions and can be delivered using commodity cloud infrastructures; therefore, many processes that rely on images can be reassessed. For example, an organisation that repairs or replaces car windscreens could use image processing to remotely assess the viability of repairing a chip in the glass as opposed to replacing the whole screen before visiting the customer to fix the chip, therefore being able to better optimise supplies and schedule time for the repair.

It is important that the technology is deployed with due regard for its social impact. Face recognition, for example, has to be handled particularly carefully, and the recent withdrawal of some large software companies from such recognition projects has highlighted the ethical concerns that need to be addressed before solutions are deployed. These very important social considerations are handled separately in this book in Chapter 11.

Speech recognition
Speech recognition is a good example of NLP in action. It enables machines to comprehend and handle human speech. It uses intricate algorithms and models, often based on neural networks and deep learning, to analyse audio input and transform spoken language into text. NLP techniques play a crucial role in enabling speech recognition systems to accurately detect words and phrases, even amid background noise or diverse accents. These systems are trained on vast datasets of labelled speech data, allowing them to learn the complex patterns and nuances of human language.

Foundation models

Unlike traditional AI systems designed for specific purposes, foundation models are more general purpose, generative and adaptable. Even though they are pre-trained, they can be fine-tuned for various applications like natural language processing, image recognition and code generation. They learn complex patterns and relationships within the data, allowing them to generate text, translate languages, write different kinds of content and answer questions. You can think of foundation models as a versatile base on which to build more specialised AI systems.

Image models, like OpenAI's CLIP, are trained to understand the relationship between images and text. Their applications include image classification, captioning, image editing and visual question and answer.

Multimodal models can understand and process different types of information referred to as modalities. For example OpenAI's DALL-E can process text to generate images. Another called ImageBind, from Facebook's owners, Meta, can work in six modalities; process text, audio, visual, thermal and inertial information. It is used to create immersive experiences.

You may be thinking of applications that are way beyond the mainstream examples described so far. If you are, you may need to look beneath the hood to see if the underlying technology can be used directly to bring your idea to life.

Key underlying technologies

The toolkits are built on underlying AI capability. This section describes how that underlying technology works and provides some pointers to more detailed material. You do not need to understand the technology to use the various toolkits on the market, but it will be useful if you need to communicate with vendors or technical teams. Each of the functional areas I have covered in the previous sections relies on three key technologies: machine learning, deep learning and big data.

- **Machine learning**. The general ability of a machine to learn from data and adapt its behaviour. In the context of this book, software systems that can predict or classify using training data and then apply that learning to real data. Neural networks are an important class of machine learning systems and are the focus in the rest of this chapter.

- **Deep learning**. An extension to machine learning in the form of multi-layer neural networks that can learn more sophisticated ways of interpreting the training data to predict an outcome. Although this appears to be a minor extension to machine learning, the combination of many additional network layers, large amounts of training data and improvements in the technology used within the network layers led a major advance in the performance of these deep learning systems in the early 2010s, and consequently brought about the advances in intelligent technology that we see today.

- **Big data**. For a deep learning system to work properly it needs to be trained using a representative amount of data. In many applications that means a very large set of data. Along with the advances in AI, the ability to store and manage very large datasets has been a key parallel technology and development. Very simple AI produces good results when fed with very large amounts of good data. The best AI will produce poor results if there are not enough data or those data are of poor quality.

These three types of technologies are used in conjunction with neural networks, so a brief explanation of how these software structures work is needed to understand why we are in the middle of such a revolution.

Neural networks

When logic no longer fuelled AI development the parallel study of neural networks took over. This field drew inspiration from biology and the structure of the brain to build machines that 'learnt' how to predict or classify without being given any information about the structure of the problem to be solved, just a large amount of training data with the expected result. Once the machine learnt to produce output that was close enough to the expected result, then it could classify or predict using actual data, as long as the training data were sufficiently representative.

A simple neural network will take a number of inputs and feed them through layers of artificial cells loosely modelled on biological neurons. Each cell takes a weighted input from the previous layer that is then aggregated with the other inputs to form an output that is fed to the following layer. The inputs are usually arrays of floating point numbers and the weight is a scaling factor which represents the importance of that input to the performance of the overall network. The larger the weight, the more the output of the cell is influenced by the input. In Figure 2.2 an input layer is connected to a single hidden layer and then that in turn is connected to an output layer with a single node. Although production systems have more layers and complexity, this is the essence of a neural network.

Figure 2.2 A simple neural network

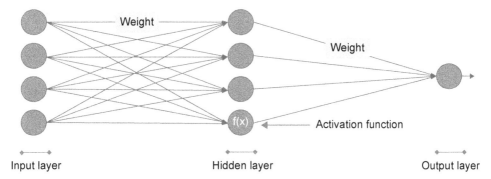

For a neural network to produce useful outputs it has to be trained by running representative data through the network and then adapting the weights on each connection between cells to achieve the best result.

Multi-layered neural networks
To find the secret to the success of neural networks and their use in deep learning, we must delve a bit further into how they work (see Figure 2.3).

Networks for deep learning are characterised by multiple layers. Anything above four layers is deemed to be in the realms of deep learning.

The first layer handles the input from the data (training, test and real data). The intermediate layers, or hidden layers, process the results of the previous layer and finally feed an output layer which provides the result that the designer is looking for, for example categorisation of an image, prediction of a result, or classification of a spoken phrase.

Figure 2.3 A multi-layered neural network

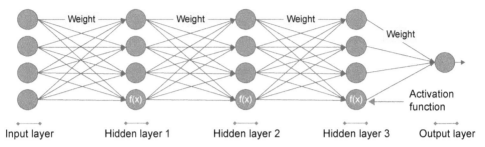

Deep learning produces such accurate results because of the interaction of the multiple layers and the training algorithms that adjust the weights. In the next sections I describe how this happens.

The role of hidden layers

The power of deep learning comes with the implementation of hidden layers. The hidden layers provide flexibility so that the whole model adapts itself to the task in hand. As long as the basic design of the network is suitable for the type of problem in hand and the training data are sufficient then the training algorithms will do the rest. The type of decisions that data scientists and engineers have to make are:

- number of layers;
- the connectedness of each layer;
- the aggregation functions (called activation functions) to use in each layer.

The number of layers   There is no consensus on a foolproof way of deciding the number of layers in a neural network for any single problem type. It may seem odd but some level of trial and error is needed. Many classification and prediction problems just require one or two hidden layers. It is probably best to start simple and add layers if the prediction results are not adequate.

Connectedness   How connected does the network have to be? You can start by saying that every cell needs to be connected to every cell in the next layer (a dense network) but this configuration uses considerable resources. Neural networks use a lot of computing power so after the first few experiments it may be beneficial to move to a sparser network.

Activation functions   For each layer, there is a choice of mathematical function that is applied to all the inputs to compute the output. The selected function is called an activation function. In practice a small number of functions are commonly used, and a surprising fact is that one of those functions, called 'ReLu' (Deep AI, n.d.), produced a step change in the ability of neural networks to find optimal solutions for real-world problems. Some researchers (Feng and Shengnan, 2019) put the recent success of deep learning down to widespread adoption of this seemingly simple function.

Training the network

Neural networks learn by adjusting the weights while running through training data. The weights are adjusted to improve the performance of the network by reducing the difference between the output of the network and the training data. This difference is called the loss and you can imagine the function relating the loss to the weights as a surface, as illustrated in Figure 2.4.

Figure 2.4 Neural networks try to minimise loss

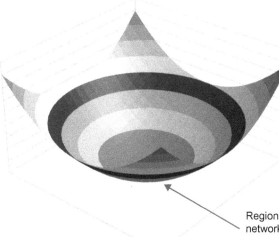

The loss function represents the difference between the prediction and the actual outcome. The neural network is trained so that the weights in all the layers are adjusted to minimise the loss function. The loss function can be represented as a bowl with each weight being one of the three dimensions.

Region in which the loss is minimised so neural networks try to adjust their weights through the training process to produce a loss as close to the bottom of the bowl as possible.

The surface will have a region where the loss takes on a minimum value, so it can be thought of as a bowl shape. In reality the surface would be uneven with many ripples and features but it does not affect the overall objective, which is to find the set of weights that minimise the loss. Put another way, we need to find our way to the bottom of the bowl from any starting point on the surface, so this is the objective of the learning process.

Loss functions and their role in guiding the learning process After each iteration, or batch of iterations, through the training data the loss function is evaluated. This function tells the machine the magnitude of the difference between its predictions and the actual results recorded in the training data. The same loss function can be used to say in which direction the weights need to be adjusted, but it does not say how much by, so that decision is left to the designer of the network (see Figure 2.5).

The practicalities of sourcing training data It is no coincidence that good results are coming from applications that can supply large amounts of data. All the large cloud platform providers have access to data on a global scale. They also get good results from their NLP, analytics, search and image classification.

In a commercial setting, as part of considering whether an AI solution can produce good results, the availability of training data and the quality of the ongoing actual data should be considered very carefully. There are many types of problems for which you do not need to provide the data because you can get toolkits that have already been trained.

Figure 2.5 Adjusting weights to minimise loss

Step 1. The slope of the bowl surface is computed at the point represented by the initial weights.

Step 2. Weights are then adjusted slightly in the direction of the bottom of the bowl.

Step 3. The loss function is then re-calculated. The overall value of the loss function should have reduced, and by repeating iterations of steps 1 to 3 the loss function will track towards the bottom of the bowl.

If you need to source your own training data then you need to make sure they are available in enough volume. Many successful AI solutions use millions of records. These data then have to be of good enough quality, and a representative sample of the information that they are representing, in order for them to be a valid training set. Developers of AI systems have started to use generative AI to create synthetic data for training purposes. Some have told me that it speeds up the process of training significantly. That said, the quality of synthetic data matters and should be handled with great care as it will affect the quality of the model itself.

If a measurement technique for one of the attributes changed halfway through the sample then the data would need some attention before they could be used for training, and this all requires expertise.

Neural networks are not difficult in concept but in practice the large amounts of data involved and the technical implementations needed to allow them to perform adequately mean there are many components and design decisions needed before a system can work in production. Luckily, the world recognised that to make this type of AI solution workable, toolkits were needed so that the people with the business problem were not faced with many detailed implementation questions.

Having delved into some of the workings of neural networks, the following sections come back up a level and describe how the technology is being packaged for business use into different types of toolkit.

Making the most out of toolkits

Vendors and organisations have surrounded the underlying technologies with toolkits that make them usable in enterprises without them having to reinvent the wheel. The huge investment in the AI market means that vendor and open-source offerings have developed to the point where there are many credible options for enterprises of all scales. In practical terms, many decisions about the use of AI technology will hinge on the vendor–toolkit–framework you wish to adopt. So here I will break down the level of tooling that is available and, depending on the type of organisation you work for, the choices that you might make. You will not need to delve into the neural networks themselves; the dashboards and configuration editors will be all you need to get the business outcome you require.

Table 2.1 summarises types of toolkit, the functionality available, the mix of team and skills that you might need and examples of how the toolkits can be used.

Table 2.1 The toolkits and the functionality available, with user examples

Type of toolkit	Examples	Functionality or use case examples	Users
Configurable business solutions			
Finance systems	Intelligent forecasting or fraud prevention, radically different conversational user interfaces	Conversational user interface, intelligence analytics and guidance on next steps	Many types of office workers, e.g. staff in the finance department, financial business analysts and staff engaged in fraud prevention in insurance, or tackling fraudulent invoicing, business analysts who can configure the intelligent features of the software for the users
HR	Recruitment solutions	CV screening	HR or recruitment analysts, business analysts who can configure the intelligent features of the software for the users

(Continued)

Table 2.1 (Continued)

Type of toolkit	Examples	Functionality or use case examples	Users
Customer relations management	Personalisation of services, customer journey and contact management, solutions for customer service agents	IVAs added to CRM solutions can provide conversational interfaces for customers, or intelligent assistants for customer service agents	Customer contact managers have these implemented by technical specialists for use by their customers and contact centre agents. Customer journey analysts can analyse the data from these interactions to design better customer journeys. A good example of this is provided in Chapter 7, the Calderdale Council case study. Business analysts can configure the intelligent features of the software for the users including agents
Toolkits for business functions			
IDP	Form interpretation and uploading, e.g. mortgage application forms	Parse and interpret text, field identification and interpretation	Toolkit configuration experts use these solutions to create products for end users such as those handling invoices, and bank account and loan application forms, or handling service support enquiries
	Unstructured document tagging	Categorisation of unstructured text, tagging text with an industry-specific lexicon	A good example of this is provided in Chapter 6, in the Siemens Global Business Services case study where support tickets are processed automatically
Virtual agents	Customer query handling	Automated responses to questions, dialogue design tools	From personal assistants on our mobile phones and devices to chatbots on websites, these can be deployed by technology and toolkit experts to provide digital services through conversational interfaces to customers, and provide data for insights and analysis to customer journey analysts, tone-of-voice experts
	Conversational user interface for forms	Conversation designer to navigate a customer through complex forms	

(Continued)

Table 2.1 (Continued)

Type of toolkit	Examples	Functionality or use case examples	Users
	Avatars or virtual character as seen in some games	While still limited to use in gaming, in future we might see more adoption of avatars to represent people, who are working remotely, at meetings	
	Mobile phone personal assistants	Facilities to allow you to integrate your offerings into existing phone personal assistants, for example adding a voice interface to an app	
	Virtual call centre agents	Dialogue design studios, integration with telephony systems, configurable NLP	
Intelligent analytics	Targeted marketing Buying habits analysis and predictions Risk analysis	Used in marketing and advertising to target specific groups of potential buyers, understand their propensity to buy a new product or service or predict risks of customers defecting to competitors or defaulting on payments	Data analysts and data scientists analyse the data and produce reports for marketeers, or provide instant analytics online to make special offers or make recommendations, e.g. 'people who bought this also bought that'. Sales and finance teams use these to increase revenue and prevent losses
IA/IPA	Process mining	Used to find process pathways in the organisation and any bottlenecks or deviations from standard operating models. It can also be used to identify opportunities for further automation.	Set up by tool configuration specialists and used by operational team leaders, process analysts and data analysts to optimise processes

(Continued)

Table 2.1 (Continued)

Type of toolkit	Examples	Functionality or use case examples	Users
		With generative AI added to some solutions, the results can be interpreted and described in natural language to speed up analysis and any necessary remedial action	
	Intelligent exception handling[1]	A virtual agent learning from humans how to handle unusual cases	
Toolkits for specific technical functions			
NLP	Libraries are available for most popular platforms. An open-source example is NLTK that runs on Python	All the popular libraries include parsing and tagging to attach a domain or project specific meaning to language segments	Data scientists with the necessary programming skills for your chosen platform
Analysis and prediction	An example is Facebook's Prophet, an open-source tool for forecasting	Configurable models, with interpretable and adjustable parameters that analysts can use to make forecasts and predictions	Data scientists with the necessary programming skills for your chosen platform
Image recognition and classification, generation and analysis	Many open-source image processing libraries Commercial utilities and web-hosted versions from the large platform companies	From a stream of images or video the tools can classify the content and recognise objects. The configuration facilities provided by the tools vary. Some are code libraries, others have configuration studios	Depending on the tool, you will probably need programmers and AI analysts if only to integrate the results of the classification or recognition into the rest of your business process. Once integrated, business users or software robots in automated processes can take advantage of it for cross-referencing

(Continued)

Table 2.1 (Continued)

Type of toolkit	Examples	Functionality or use case examples	Users
			information or object recognition, e.g. identifying weeds in fields of food crops, taking stock on supermarket shelves, counting items in a delivery pack or checking identity, e.g. as used by governments in passport and driving licence applications
Analysis for process optimisation and exception handling	AI reconciliation platforms, automated break processing in financial services, process mining and IA/IPA tools	Functionality is changing rapidly. Tools help to define the new optimised processes based on existing usage and data. Exceptions are increasingly automated	Business analysts will be needed with both process and technical skills, the nature of which will be largely specific to the toolkit selected. When this type of software is configured, it can be used by team leaders, subject matter experts, people in charge of process efficiency and optimisation. In future the processes might become intelligent by analysing their own insights and optimise themselves to run better or to adapt to changing requirements e.g. peaks and troughs of demand

1   Exceptions are cases that automations cannot handle due to complexity or ambiguity of the information associated with them or simply that are too sensitive to be handled by machines, for example cases of bereavement.

There are a few sector-specific resources available too. Examples include QuantConnect (www.quantconnect.com/) for trading in financial markets and NVIDIA Clara (www.nvidia.com/en-gb/clara/) for AI-powered medical imaging, genomics and drug discovery.

There are other collaborative community-based platforms, like Hugging Face, that straddle function specific toolkits and foundation models. They provide spaces for AI enthusiasts to share and discover open-source models, datasets and tools, fostering innovation and accelerating development in machine learning and natural language processing. They offer a space for learning, experimentation and knowledge exchange, democratising access to cutting-edge AI resources.

Foundation models

So you have reviewed what your application vendors can supply and looked at toolkits tied to a particular functional area but the business transformation you have planned needs more. The next step to consider is to customise some of the foundation models for your organisation's use. This is already happening with custom versions of GPT LLM, for example. Organisations are licensing it and feeding it their own information to use as a general purpose chatbot for finding and retrieving information in their organisation, for example finding the relevant documents that a customer service agent might need, or answering questions about fixing a product fault based on the design and manufacturing documents of the product fed to the GPT. The Siemens Global Business Services (GBS) case study in Chapter 6 highlights the application of a customised version of GPT in handling customer enquiries in a global shared services setting.

Key underlying technologies provided by general frameworks

If the foundation models do not answer all your needs either, then it is worth considering one of the key underlying technology frameworks that are supplied by the large platform vendors, the big open-source projects and the new challengers.

If you want your AI investment to build a lasting differentiation against your competitors or to disrupt a market then this is probably where you want to be. In this section I provide pointers for you to follow with some comments. The market is moving so fast that no printed list will be current for long so here I shamelessly point to web resources.

I love generalised frameworks. To make use of them you will need a team of data scientists. This is a much more specialist skill set than the business analyst who might configure the toolkits above. Maybe you have a team of data scientists already in place, but if not, then it will be the people, not the technology, that dominate your spend if you adopt a generalised framework to build your own competitive advantage.

All the major platform players offer frameworks that can be used to create and manage neural networks including:

- TensorFlow from Google.
- Microsoft's Azure AI Services.
- PyTorch sponsored by Facebook.
- Keras.
- Amazon SageMaker on Amazon Web Services (AWS).
- Apple's Intelligence in conjunction with its on-device Apple Neural Engine (ANE).

Each of these frameworks is different in nature and those differences will steer your choices. If you start going down this route you will need to evaluate each of these and more against your project objectives. The choice of framework is important because once you have invested in a framework you will not want to change quickly.

Path to success

With such dramatic results being achieved by the best AI projects the rewards are high. Needless to say, there are significant risks as well. Here are my lessons on the path to success with AI, learnt from my research, the case studies in this book and other customer engagements:

1. Some of the technology is new and quite complex so keep your implementation as simple as it can be while proving that your objective can be realised.

2. Either use simple AI with a very large amount of data (e.g. likelihood of customer defection)...

3. ...or use a toolkit to encapsulate the complexity and use a team who are close to the business sponsors to configure high-value quick wins. Simple virtual agents to take the load off call centre staff and IDP to automate the handling of forms with unstructured text are both good examples.

4. Generative AI tools like ChatGPT offer great opportunities to augment your information workers. First identify who can benefit from the tools by assessing the kind of work that they do. For example, it can help customer contact agents with quick summaries of customer activity so that they can interact with the customer effectively or produce nicely worded reply emails to them. Or your marketing team could get a boost from the tools' ability to produce content for your website and sales brochures. Almost all your teams could benefit from automated meeting note generation, summarisation of key points or translation where necessary.

5. If you need to differentiate your business by custom-building your own neural networks then recognise that payroll costs will dominate your investment because you will need a team to build and continuously evolve the solution.

These general paths to success then require management action to support them.

Management considerations

Apart from the technical aspects to these transformation projects, there are important management actions that business and organisation leaders should consider to support their innovation initiatives:

1. Strategies to manage disruption in your own market.

2. Organisational changes to address the challenges of AI.

3. Changes to IT and vendor strategies.

I will cover each of these in the following sections.

Market disruption

Managing a business through disruptive times is difficult. It almost certainly means placing some bets beyond the traditional comfort zone of the decision-makers. Those aspects of your business that most differentiate you in your marketplace are probably a good place to start, with some experiments that will possibly involve limited investment but significant commitment from internal and external personnel, such as your subject matter experts and consultants with AI implementation skills.

Based on the case studies in this book, and successful adopters of AI, the advice is to start several radical projects and fail early. Those that succeed could be your growth drivers through this wave of change.

Organisational change

Once you get a feel for the type of change your business needs to make, then consider the implications for your organisation. New ways of thinking and new interfaces with stakeholders need the correct organisational structure to support them. New roles will include data scientists who look at internal and external information and can work with others in your organisation to see new possibilities. Human interface designers will be able to project the right tone and image through dialogues and avatars.

It is very important to assess your organisation's current state and ask:

- Does your organisation want to move out of its comfort zone and embrace new business models?

- Can you challenge the current state and think of radical new futures for your organisation?

- Does your organisation have the skills to investigate new solutions, particularly in data science?

- Can you recast the human interface with customers, employees and other stakeholders?

Others have found that having decided on an approach, organisational changes are needed to empower the new roles of AI analysts and data scientists. AI analysts ensure that the end-to-end interaction between the AI implementation and the stakeholders achieves the planned objectives. Data scientists forge the links between the available information and the learning systems. Depending on the scope of your deployments, these roles might represent individuals or large teams but they are relatively new skill sets and will require the organisational structure to change if they are to be empowered to make the necessary changes in IT and operational departments.

IT and vendor strategy

AI and its associated technologies have changed the IT market. Further changes will follow as the many hundreds of toolkits jostle for dominance. You will probably need to forge relationships with a few of the toolkit vendors to support sufficient innovation in your projects as you blaze a trail for your organisation. At the same time your traditional vendors can probably offer safer alternative, if slower, paths, and so they too need to be brought on board with your thinking.

SUMMARY

In this chapter I provided a brief overview of the science behind the, currently, most dominant approach to AI using neural networks. For context, I provided some of the history of the main developments, some of which are really quite technical. The good news is that, for most of us, that technical detail can be accessed using 'toolkits' which provide the functionality we need without exposing us to the inner workings of AI. These toolkits are themselves rapidly evolving so I put forward a classification that should help select those that you want to work with.

For readers who want to understand a bit more about neural networks, I went on to explain how these structures work. Some remarkable results can be obtained with relatively simple neural networks. Nonetheless, it is the incorporation of this technology into the context of every enterprise that holds the promise of rapid advances. At the end of the chapter I discussed some of the matters that managers should consider about the broader organisational implications of AI. This sets the scene for the next chapters in this part of the book, in which I look at generative AI, and the impact of AI on innovation and efficiency.

3   GENERATIVE AI

In November 2022, OpenAI made an instance of its large language model (LLM), ChatGPT-3.5, available to the public for free. It took the world by storm thanks to its wide ranging advanced capabilities that saw a jaw-dropping 1 million people subscribe to it within five days of its launch – by far the fastest adoption of any technology to date. ChatGPT-3.5 can answer questions and provide information on virtually any topic based on its extensive training on books, public sources of information, internet content, and data sets, up to January 2022. Its capabilities include brainstorming ideas, generating, editing and proofreading text, offering advice, engaging in storytelling, playing games and puzzles, and help with coding and programming.

ChatGPT is generative AI in that it can generate new digital content like text. In this chapter, I explore generative AI, largely focusing on large language models as one of its key enablers, as well as its issues such as hallucinations. I also cover the importance of the prompt and the emerging field of prompt engineering. I provide more examples of multimodal AI as well. Throughout the chapter I highlight how these developments enrich the automated capabilities that benefit enterprises in different ways.

SEEING IS BELIEVING: THE MAGIC OF CHATGPT

ChatGPT-3.5 plainly demonstrates the potential of conversational AI to all. When it was released by OpenAI, it led to a wave of articles estimating the impact of the technology on the world economy. McKinsey, for example, highlighted the immense economic potential of generative AI in a report titled *The Economic Potential of Generative AI: The Next Productivity Frontier* published in June 2023. In the report, it estimated that generative AI could contribute between $2.6 trillion and $4.4 trillion annually across the 63 use cases analysed in the report (Chui et al., 2023). To put this into perspective, that's akin to adding a new country the size and economic productivity of the United Kingdom to the global economy. This contribution could increase the total impact of all AI technologies by 15–40 per cent.

OpenAI has since released ChatGPT-4, and ChatGPT-4o. These are more powerful than ChatGPT-3.5 and are members of a family of products powered by OpenAI's GPT-4 LLM. They are multimodal AI, meaning they can process different kinds of input, for example text, images and audio, in real time.

Just as OpenAI is releasing more advanced and powerful LLMs to the market, so are its rivals, such as Google with its Gemini LLM. There is truly an AI model arms-race style of competition going on that is leading to faster development of the technology.

DEFINITIONS

Generative AI

Generative AI is a broad category of artificial intelligence with the primary function of generating original content in the form of text, images, music and videos. To do so different generative AI solutions tap various types of AI models, like LLMs, based on their main focus area. For example, DALL-E, which is OpenAI's image-from-text-generating AI, uses transformers and other models to generate images. It is trained on a large dataset of text–image pairs, learning to map between textual descriptions and visual representations.

Large language models

ChatGPT is based on GPT LLMs, but it is not the only one on the market. Others include Google's Gemini, xAI's Grok, Meta's LLaMA, Anthropic's Claude, Mistral AI's models, and Databricks' DBRX. In addition, Microsoft Copilot is based on OpenAI ChatGPT.

LLMs are good at both generating human-quality text and handling other natural language processing tasks like classifying information. Through massive amounts of training data, LLMs learn the relationships between words, allowing them to grasp the nuances of language, including syntax (sentence structure) and semantics (meaning). To describe the capabilities of their LLMs, AI technology vendors often quote the number of parameters in a model and the tokens in the context window.

Parameters

Parameters are the model's internal controls, allowing it to learn and optimise its responses. By adjusting the parameters based on its training data, a model learns the best way to analyse information to produce the required output. An example of a parameter is weight, which was discussed in Chapter 2 in the context of neural networks. Weight is a parameter in LLMs too. Other LLM parameters include embedding, which helps the LLM understand the meaning of words and phrases.

Context window

A context window is where the focus of an interaction is with an LLM or the length of the text in a conversation. The length of the context window is a combination of the prompt and the previous conversation up to a limit, to enable the LLM to understand what is needed and relevant to the response that it produces. For example, if you give an LLM a large document to read, it will focus on the most recent text in the document that falls within its context window. The larger the window the better the LLM at understanding context, nuances and instructions – therefore processing instructions with better accuracy. The flip side is that more computing power is required to process larger context windows and so the response can be slower. The context window size is often described in terms of tokens.

Tokens

Tokenisation is used to break text into smaller units called tokens. A token is therefore the fundamental unit of text. Tokens can be complete words like cat or tree or a portion of a word, for instance, swim taken from swimming. Tokens can also be single characters like full stops and commas.

LLMs use tokenisation to process text. It allows them to apply rules to produce meaningful outputs. The tokens serve as the essential building blocks that allow LLMs to effectively process and understand text. The more tokens an LLM can process in its context window, the better it becomes at remembering longer conversations, and handling context and nuances.

The importance of the prompt

LLMs can generate text by predicting the next token or word in the context of the subject. The subject is in the instruction that we give them and that is known as the prompt. How LLMs are prompted is important and affects the quality of the output. The more specific and precise the prompt, the better the LLM output.

In Table 3.1, several examples demonstrate the power of the prompt. How it is written can make a big difference to the output of an LLM – Google's Gemini in this case. The below prompts ask Gemini to explain how tides work using various themes:

1. In scientific terms.
2. In Shakespearean language.
3. In plain language so that a six-year-old would understand.
4. In 'street lingo'.

The length and styles of the generated output speak for themselves.

Table 3.1 Prompts driving different styles of output from the free version of Google Gemini but explaining the same thing

Prompt (instruction)	Gemini output
Can you explain tides scientifically in 200 words?	Tides arise from the interplay of gravitational forces between Earth, the Moon and, to a lesser extent, the Sun. The Moon's gravity exerts a stronger pull on the side of Earth facing it, causing the water to bulge outward.
	However, Earth isn't rigid. The centrifugal force arising from Earth's rotation counteracts gravity slightly on the far side, creating another bulge. These bulges correspond to high tides. Conversely, regions between the bulges experience low tides due to a relative weakening of the gravitational pull.
	The Sun's gravity also plays a part, though weaker. When the Sun and Moon's gravitational pulls align (full and new moon), their combined effect creates higher high tides and lower low tides

(Continued)

Table 3.1 (Continued)

Prompt (instruction)	Gemini output
	(spring tides). Conversely, when their pulls are at right angles (first and third quarter moon), the opposing effects result in smaller tidal variations (neap tides).
	Therefore, tides are a complex interplay of gravitational forces and Earth's rotation, resulting in the rhythmic rise and fall of ocean waters.
Can you explain tides in 200 words in the style of Shakespeare?	Hark! A tale of the ocean's restless heart, a dance of forces played by moon's soft art. Diana, goddess pale, with silvered grace, doth weave a spell upon this watery space.
	Her gentle pull, a cosmic hand unseen, draws forth the seas in mountains vast and keen. A swelling tide, on shores by Luna kissed, where waves do rise in grandeur, tempest-kissed.
	Yet hold! Earth turns, a globe in constant flight, and on the far side, too, the waters fight. For though Diana's grasp may seem more faint, Earth's whirling dance a counterforce doth paint.
	Thus twice a day, the ocean doth confess, to Luna's might, a watery wilderness. With rhythmic sighs, it ebbs and flows anew, a testament to forces old and true.
	The Sun, too, joins this cosmic ballet's grace, with lesser pull, yet leaving still its trace. When Sun and Moon in harmony combine, the tides they swell, a sight both fierce and fine.
	But when their pulls in opposition stand, a gentler rise and fall across the land. So mark the moon, dear friend, and understand, the ocean's breath is ruled by her command.
Can you explain tides in plain language so that a six-year-old would understand, in no more than 100 words?	The ocean is like a giant bathtub, and the moon is a giant ball pulling on all that water. As the moon goes around Earth, the water gets pulled in different directions, making big bulges. Those bulges are high tides! When the bulge is on the other side of Earth, the water gets pulled away, making the ocean seem lower – that's low tide! So, the moon plays tug-of-war with the ocean, making it rise and fall like waves on a super slow beach!
Can you describe tides in street lingo in 100 words?	Yo, the ocean's like a massive pool, right? The moon's this big dude in the sky, pullin' on all that water. So as the moon zooms around Earth, the water gets yanked in different directions, makin' big bumps. Those bumps are high tide, like the pool's overflowin'! When the moon's on the other side, the water gets pulled away, so the beach gets extra exposed – that's low tide, dude! Basically, the moon's playin' tug-of-war with the ocean, makin' it rise and fall like a super chill wave.

Prompt engineering

As illustrated in Table 3.1, prompts can make a big difference to the outputs of LLMs. This is why prompt engineering has become an important field in its own right. In fact, prompt engineers, by fine-tuning the prompting, can get the language model to provide new functionality; for example, become a specialist in summarising the key points from large online documents, like extracting the most important points from the text of new legislation. Prompt engineering is an iterative task that entails rewording the prompt again and again to see which version produces the best output. Prompt engineers need to have a good knowledge and understanding of the model architecture, parameters, and its training. It is an emerging field with huge potential for the future of AI. The better the prompt the better the answer from the LLM.

Multimodal generative AI

Generative AI offerings can be multimodal; that is, they can use different models to analyse and process text, data, audio, video, produce images from text and more.

Transformers

The 'transformer' architecture that powers generative AI was a breakthrough dating back to 2017. Transformers use a technique, referred to as self-attention, to understand complex relationships between different words, leading to the kind of impressive responses that they produce today.

Self-attention

Self-attention is the core mechanism that powers transformers by allowing them to understand relationships between different words or phrases in text by considering the whole context rather than just the nearby words. Essentially, through self-attention, the model is engaging in a dialogue with itself, questioning what actions it should take and which words in the sentence hold the most significance for its objectives. By considering how the words relate to each other, the model can develop a better understanding of the whole sentence, therefore gaining the ability to focus on what matters the most within the sentence.

Although it's widely used in language models, self-attention also benefits other fields like computer vision and speech recognition by helping models grasp broader relationships and context.

One issue with self-attention is that it can lead to errors that have become known as 'hallucinations'. This can be for various reasons such as overfitting, or noisy or contradictory examples in its training data that lead to the wrong associations, or relying on the surrounding context that can be ambiguous or insufficient. An LLM might then make up content to fill the gap.

Overfitting happens when an algorithm closely fits its training data, consequently reducing the model's ability to predict anything that does not match its training data. When a model using self-attention overfits, it tends to produce results that are too closely tied to the specific details and biases in the training data, instead of working well with new inputs. Hallucinations and errors are discussed in more detail later in this chapter.

For a more detailed explanation of transformers, please refer to the paper titled 'Attention is all you need' published by Google (Vaswani et al., 2017).

Image and video creation

As mentioned before, generative AI is not just about text and language processing using LLMs. The term refers to the use of a variety of models to generate other digital assets like images and videos. Take ChatGPT as an example. It is part of a family of generative AI that includes DALL-E, the image generator. An example of DALL-E's output is shown in Figure 3.1. This was produced on my prompt to generate an image of a city through time becoming more futuristic. I asked for a bendy road in the image as a symbol of enterprises' journeys to becoming autonomous.

There are already many technology vendors that offer text to video generation too. The big generative AI players, namely Google and OpenAI, have their own offerings called Veo and Sora respectively.

Figure 3.1 A DALL-E-generated image of a city through time

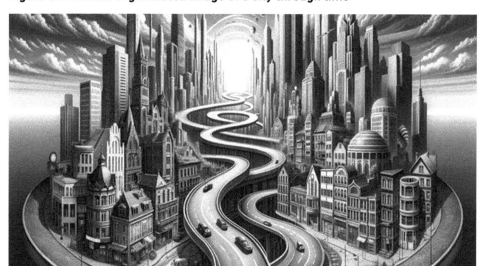

Generative AI errors and hallucinations

Machine learning (ML) and deep learning (DL) (a sub-category of ML) are based on statistical analysis. As such they are probabilistic not deterministic. With deterministic systems you can be sure that given inputs A and B you get output C. A calculator or a vending machine are good examples. With a calculator you know that when you type in the numbers that you want to add up, the calculator gives you the correct sum. With a vending machine, you know that when you pay the right amount of money for a product and tap its code into the machine, that product will drop off the rack and be delivered to you, barring any mechanical failures.

ML and DL systems are different in that they work on probabilities. They basically give you the answers that they have calculated to have the highest probability of being correct – and that might not always be the case. The accuracy of their answers depends on a number of factors including their design, any biases in the data that they were trained on and how much training they were given. An example of bias in data is ML being fed images of men in scrubs labelled as doctors and women in similar garb labelled as nurses. If the AI is then asked to guess the job of a woman doctor from her photo where she is dressed in the typical scrubs, the AI will guess a nurse and not a doctor. Unsurprisingly, if asked to guess the job of a male nurse similarly attired, the AI would say a doctor.

Developers of ML and DL systems use a variety of ways to reduce the probability of errors including using large sample sizes for training data, but errors can still occur.

Under the hood, generative AI is based on DL and ML. It uses statistical analysis for processing information and can make errors. Some errors have become known as hallucinations. Hallucinations occur when a mix of design, gaps in training and prompt issues lead to the AI making mistakes or making things up.

When ChatGPT-3.5 took the world by storm in November 2022, many of us took to testing it, and there were reports of people who had been able to fool it into giving the wrong answers to simple sums, or come up with legal precedence that never existed, and other issues that quickly became known as hallucinations.

I had first-hand experience of a generative AI hallucination when in answer to my question about the first ever dive to Challenger Deep, the deepest point in the Pacific Ocean, the software mixed up Jacques Piccard who did the dive, with Jacques Cousteau, the French oceanic explorer, and their respective dives. Only by checking the answer further and referencing other sources of information was I able to separate the facts from the fiction that it had generated.

The prompt plays a crucial role in ensuring that generative AI provides outputs that are relevant and correct. For example, if you ask generative AI to summarise a long article for you, it might give you a summary of the subject of the article but not the key points. To ensure that you get a summary of the key points from the article you have to specifically ask it to list a summary of the key points in the article.

Retrieval-augmented generation

Large context windows help reduce errors and hallucinations. Another way to deal with the issues is retrieval-augmented generation (RAG). RAG is a technique used to improve the accuracy of generative AI responses. It works by bringing together information retrieval from external sources with LLMs. Like a guide, RAG provides generative AI with access to reliable external sources of information such as knowledge repositories or online databases. The AI searches the sources for information in the context of the prompt. It then uses the prompt and the retrieved information to create a more relevant and accurate response than it could have done without RAG.

The use of RAG improves the likelihood of the response being correct, reducing the risks of errors and hallucinations. Maintaining information repositories for RAG is important as poor information life-cycle management affects the outcomes, with stale documents and intranet site content, defeating the objective of using RAG.

APPLICATIONS OF GENERATIVE AI IN THE ENTERPRISE

In this section I recap and further explore the fundamental capabilities of generative AI and its applications in the enterprise. The core capabilities of generative AI are outlined below.

Natural language processing (NLP)

A language-focused generative AI has NLP techniques at its heart. As such it can understand and generate human-like text. Its understanding is different from human understanding because it does not comprehend the meaning of words but their relationship to each other and the sentence structure based on statistical analysis and its training. Generative AI takes NLP further in that it can create content, summarise and translate information, do sentiment analysis and converse with humans to produce context-based text in response to prompts.

Image and video generation

Different types of generative AI can create realistic images, videos and animations from scratch or enhance existing visual content. This includes everything from generating photorealistic images to producing animated videos that can be used in marketing and entertainment.

Data synthesis and augmentation

Besides generative AI's NLP and image and video generation capabilities, it can also create synthetic data to augment and enhance existing datasets. Data synthesis is being used by developers to train machine learning models, where the quality and quantity of data significantly impact performance. That said, training AI models exclusively on synthetic data generated by prior models poses significant risks to the model. There are reports of experiments that demonstrated the potential for model collapse, a phenomenon where the AI's performance progressively deteriorates, leading to increasingly nonsensical and inaccurate outputs (Shumailov et al., 2024). This degradation stems from issues like feedback loops that amplify existing biases and errors within the model. As new models learn from flawed synthetic data, these imperfections become entrenched, further distorting the AI's understanding of reality. This underscores the importance of incorporating diverse and representative real-world data during training to ensure the robustness and reliability of AI models.

Analytics

Generative AI can complement analytics, for example, to tap unstructured data for analysis and also explain the findings of analytics in natural language.

GENERATIVE AI USE CASES IN THE ENTERPRISE

Given its capabilities generative AI has a variety of applications in the enterprise. A selection of them are described in the following sections.

Personalisation and customisation

Generative AI can be used to produce personalised content and experiences for individual users or customers. It can do so by using the analysis of their preferences and past behaviour and then generating the content. This capability significantly boosts personalised marketing campaigns and product recommendations to customers. It can also enrich other capabilities. For example, media streaming services use generative AI to enhance their recommendations to their customers. They use recommendation engines combined with generative AI to provide good summaries and rich textual output for recommendations that enhance the user experience.

Design, prototyping and creativity

Generative AI can support and boost creative processes by engaging in design discussions and conceptualisation. It can give a helping hand with design and creativity through means such as brainstorming, market data insights and converting ideas into images, for example, of what a product would look like. It can convert text to images and videos and music as well. I talk more about this in Chapter 4: AI for Innovation, including music generation.

To show the power of generative AI in innovation and creativity I asked ChatGPT-4o to help me design a product to help elderly folks, who have no access to the web, deal with digital services. ChatGPT-4o came up with a product name, its key features and the services that would be required to support it. Then it produced a collage image of all the components of the proposed solution. You can read the content of my entire conversation with ChatGPT-4o on this subject in Chapter 4.

Business process automation

Generative AI increases the scope of automation of business processes in the enterprise. We have been able to automate repetitive tasks such as data entry and reading of text and documents for some years now. Today, generative AI enables us to also automate content creation, report generation and many aspects of document processing, such as identifying the key points from a document, summarising and translating it.

Generative AI can help the creative processes in the organisation too. These are also business processes; for example, creating content for websites and marketing material that today can be partly automated with AI.

The power of automation is being tapped in industries that have previously benefited less from digitalisation than others. Examples include consultancies that are using generative AI to create proposals and quotes, legal firms that are using it to get summaries of long legal documents, and estate agents that are able to automate production of sales materials for their stock of properties.

Another example is generative AI used to create the framework for discussions and brainstorming sessions, as well as content for training materials. Its language abilities go beyond producing text because it can also be used to proofread and improve text, and make sure that articles and blogs are optimised for search.

Insight generation and analytics

AI can extract meaningful insights from large datasets, providing advanced analytics that support decision-making. This includes identifying trends, uncovering hidden patterns and generating detailed reports.

With generative AI, you can add virtual assistance agents that draw on such analysis of information to help guide users on a variety of topics; for example, to take the next best action in a process or when handling a customer call. Generative AI can work out how to improve that process, for example based on productivity and task mining intelligence.

Custom enterprise LLMs

LLMs can be licensed by enterprises for their internal use. The approach is to license the required LLM, like GPT from OpenAI. Then isolate it from the web and train it in your required enterprise content. By isolating it from the web, enterprises ensure that the LLM's knowledge remains within the realm of the organisation cut off from outside influences and misinformation. The LLM can then be used to help employees find answers to their work-related questions drawn from the corporate information repositories and systems.

Interactive and conversational agents

With generative AI the development of chatbots and virtual assistants has become a lot easier. The technology enables interactive and human-like conversations based on content and data analysis. These agents can handle customer enquiries, provide support, and facilitate transactions. A good example is that of the Siemens Global Business Services Bionic Agent in the case study in Chapter 6 which has recently been augmented with generative AI.

The industry giants like Microsoft and Google are adding more and more virtual assistant features to their personal productivity tools, for example Microsoft Copilot, to help those who use these applications to become more productive.

Language translation and localisation

Documents can be automatically translated into other languages using generative AI. This functionality of generative AI is a boon to enterprises that often have to translate business documents and other content, such as marketing blurb, into different languages. Imagine having instant translation and localisation of text that you might post on your corporate website, designed for different parts of the world, or error messages in software code, designed for users in different countries. Automated translation would significantly speed up deployments.

INDUSTRY EXAMPLES OF APPLICATIONS OF GENERATIVE AI

I have covered a number of horizontal applications of generative AI above. Here I provide some examples of its vertical applications:

- In healthcare generative AI can help with explaining conditions in simple language, demystifying clinical terminology for patients and their families.

- In clinical trials generative AI can be used to automate report creation based on the results of research and explaining the outcomes. Consequently, it can free up researchers from some administrative duties, allowing them to focus on the more critical aspects of clinical trials.

- In the travel industry generative AI can help with planning tours and itineraries with recommendations based on customer preferences.

- In logistics generative AI can power chatbots for customer support and order tracking. Using a conversational interface, it can tap live traffic data to advise delivery drivers of alternative routes to avoid traffic jams and road closures in real time, ensuring timely deliveries.

GENERATIVE AI RISKS AND CHALLENGES

As I marvel at the possibilities that generative AI presents today, I cannot stop thinking about the risks that it brings. One of the biggest risks that I am seeing is its hasty adoption by enterprises simply to have the latest new shiny thing. For example, friends tell me that the translation jobs market in publishing has shrunk significantly since the world learnt the potential of generative AI. And I know from my own experience of working with generative AI that its output in English needs reviewing and editing. I wonder how much time and effort has gone into assessing its translation output and if too many humans have been taken out of the loop in pursuit of cost savings. Another factor to consider is that the training has been focused on the English language. This affects its translation to and from other languages where its training is not to the same standard that we see in English.

Or perhaps it is the nature of jobs in translation that is changing from actually doing the translation to supervising and checking the output of generative AI. Then doing what it cannot do, like translating dialects.

The elephant in the room is the impact of generative AI on all jobs, not just in publishing. In Chapter 11: Automation and Society, I delve deeper into this topic.

Then there is the potential for bland and formulaic text being generated automatically that deprives the world of personal writing style. This can be overcome through prompt engineering but only if we humans ensure it is done. Otherwise, it would not be long before personal styles disappear, depriving generative AI of any examples to follow, purely as a consequence of us becoming over-dependent on it.

What impact will there be on our abilities to be creative without the help of generative AI? Will we become so dependent on it that we lose the power to be creative on our own?

On the subject of dependence on generative AI, in February 2024, Gartner, the industry analyst firm, predicted that by 2027 an enterprise's generative AI chatbot will cause the death of a customer from bad information that it provides (Fisher, 2024). It listed hallucinations as the prime reason with nonsensical or untruthful information. The death would be as a consequence of humans becoming over-reliant and dependent on authentic sounding chatbots, leading to a user's inability to separate facts from fiction and potentially risky advice.

The increase in consumption of energy and natural resources due to the increase in demand for computation is another issue with generative AI, but it could be offset by the efficiency that it generates in knowledge work. A study is needed to establish the net effect of development and use of generative AI versus the efficiencies that it generates in the enterprise. This could be significant, given that there are hundreds of millions of knowledge workers in the world.

Other risks of generative AI include its malicious use to spread misinformation to cause chaos and havoc in society. For example, generating fake videos of disasters to cause panic and looting.

It could impersonate people and their voices, increasing the threat of cybercrime. The answer is governance, a professional code of ethics, best practice and regulation. Regulation is needed today not tomorrow when it might be too late. I cover the risks and the need for inter-governmental action and regulation in more detail in Chapter 11.

SUMMARY

In this chapter I have explored the exciting technological development that is generative AI. I have covered its key features, incredible potential, and applications in the enterprise. I have provided examples of its use cases in various industries. There is more on its ability to help humans with innovation in Chapter 4: AI for Innovation.

I have also covered its potential risks and issues such as hallucinations, and its malicious use. I encourage you to learn more about it, trialling it to experience its power for yourselves, and contributing to its development, as well as risk mitigation strategies.

I highlight the many different aspects of generative AI – its capabilities, applications and risks – in the rest of the book in the relevant chapters, starting with its power to boost innovation in the next chapter.

4　AI FOR INNOVATION

In this chapter I explore how AI is proving to be a catalyst for innovation in a business environment.

First I ask why AI is so important in innovation. I then go on to look at how it can be used to look for opportunities to innovate. For example, can it be used to identify an unmet demand in a marketplace?

AI can help to generate new ideas, enable disruptive business models and enhance many types of product and services. Furthermore, there is a place within the innovation cycle for creativity in the usual artistic sense, and AI is already contributing to these activities as well. I discuss this in more detail later in this chapter.

The number and breadth of AI announcements have risen sharply since ChatGPT was released and made a huge impression on opinion formers well beyond the IT industry. The sheer volume of AI news can be overwhelming so I take a systematic approach to thinking through which innovations might apply to specific business contexts.

For many of us, the organisation for which we work gives us boundaries. We might have a great idea but it really does not fit our organisation. To turn the subject on its head, I look at an approach for identifying innovations within a constrained business context. Most organisations have plenty of problems that need imaginative solutions but they are not blank canvases. I use a generally acceptable definition of innovation to look at business models, markets, products and services. To make the discussion more concrete, I use an example of a business with a few typical business challenges and I suggest an approach to finding the most promising innovation that would work within normal project constraints.

To fuel some further ideas, I look at combinations of technologies. That is, AI working in combination with other technologies that will allow a step change in potential benefits. This, in combination with a comparison between sectors, gives a range of ideas, concepts and solutions that can apply to your organisation. I back up each combination with an example from around the world.

Finally, I look at some of the ways AI is being used in the creative industries for generating art, music, designs and sketches. These capabilities could soon extend your products or service, but even if this is not a possibility, the field of AI in the creative arts is interesting for anyone who wants to see where innovations in 5 or 10 years will come from. With generative AI already new visualisations of products and ways of thinking about services have emerged.

Before we begin looking at specific business scenarios, it is worth pausing to ask why AI is a catalyst for so much innovation. The best answer is that it is a so-called 'general purpose technology' that ranks alongside the advent of the digital computer, and World Wide Web, as written about in *The Impact of Artificial Intelligence on Innovation* published by the National Bureau of Economic Research in 2018 (Cockburn et al., 2018). This has led to the expectation that it will impact many aspects of our business and personal lives to the same degree as the personal computer, mobile phone or the web, and that AI in turn will bring about a faster pace of change because of four key factors:

- **Funding**: the capital markets are now more alive to AI's capabilities than ever before, so funds have been diverted to drive further research. There are many announcements and estimates of the amount of money being poured into the industry. The S&P Global data that I shared in Chapter 1 show that:

  - Private equity and venture capital-backed investments in generative AI companies more than doubled in 2023, reaching $2.18 billion, compared to $1 billion in 2022. This growth defied the overall slowdown in M&A (mergers and acquisitions) activity.

  - Investment peaked in the third quarter of 2023, reaching $927.7 million, a significant increase from the $121.5 million recorded in the same period in 2022.

  - The momentum continued into 2024, with $250 million invested in generative AI in the first two weeks of the year, exceeding the total for the first quarter of 2023.

- **Technology**: deep learning is now key to eye-catching developments like powerful models and neural network architectures such as transformers that power generative AI, as well as products like autonomous cars that connect with a wide population of opinion formers. It is no longer in the laboratories classifying pictures of cats.

- **Innovation**: AI is a tool for innovation in its own right. It can be thought of as an invention that is a method of invention so is difficult to dismiss or pigeonhole as 'not for us'.

- **Ubiquity**: the greater ubiquity in our everyday lives raises awareness among private and public sector decision-makers.

These drivers and others are leading to a snowball effect and the expectation that AI can address some of society's biggest issues: managing an ageing population; the transition to low carbon energy; better governance; and better-quality education. Not only can AI contribute to the solution to some of these long-term problems, it can also contribute to the process of innovation itself. That is, identifying and selecting ideas that will solve a problem. This is where I start the discussion in this chapter: how to harness AI to address identifiable wants and needs. I then look at a typical innovation cycle within a business and see how AI is contributing to different business models, processes, products and changing markets.

In many cases, the greatest opportunities for short-term innovation come from combining AI technology with other existing facilities or processes. A discipline that is moving at lightning pace is video games technology. AI is already part of many games and, in this chapter, we explore how some of the platforms and toolkits can be used in the world of corporate IT.

Research and recent generative AI developments show how AI can go further to contribute to the creative process. Experimental research in art, writing and abstract reasoning show how AI can enhance the human capacity to look at the world in a different way and, in doing so, open up new possibilities. How this research can be harnessed in business is a leading-edge topic. Maybe readers of this book will consult some of the references and go on to pioneer new solutions and ideas. In the meantime, I am going to start by looking at AI-enhanced innovation in a corporate environment.

APPLYING AI TO INNOVATION IN YOUR BUSINESS

Let's start with defining what we mean by innovation in a corporate environment. This definition from TechTarget (Pratt and McLaughlin, 2023) is practical and to the point so I have chosen to use it for this chapter:

> Business innovation is an organisation's process for introducing new ideas, workflows, methodologies, services or products. The cycle is often broken down into four parts. It starts with articulating ideas around key areas (business models, marketing, process, products and service).

So, I will start with a discussion about generating ideas in the first place, then look at how AI can contribute to innovation of business models, markets, processes and finally products and services.

Generating ideas

Business innovation of any type usually falls into one of two categories: new ways of dealing with existing requirements; or ways to satisfy an unrecognised need.

AI can help by looking at customer behaviour in ways that are very difficult with a human mind because we cannot see the patterns in very large amounts of data. If you have access to large enough datasets then you can, potentially uniquely, find customer behaviour patterns that will allow you to change your business model, marketing, processes, products or services.

Here are six ways that AI and deep learning can help you to spark ideas in your organisation.

- Finding the opportunity in a mass of data to improve something: one example is to use deep learning to spot how your customers are behaving over large populations or over long periods of time. Can you detect when a customer will defect to the competition? Can you understand the patterns of behaviour before they adopt or abandon your product or service?

- Ideation is a big part of innovation. Recent advances in generative AI are helping humans with testing out ideas, through brainstorming, applications of creative techniques, content creation, feedback and iteration, and tools and resource suggestions. I'll cover this point in more detail in the next section.

- Product usage: if you collect feedback on the way that products are used, for example white goods, energy products, or anything online, then what is it telling you about how the product or customer experience can radically change?

- Abstract reasoning: this is still a research topic in AI, but the discussion in this chapter on how deep learning can approach abstract learning shows that associating concepts and linking ideas can lead to new approaches for solving existing problems.

- Combining AI with other solutions: these are often other information processing solutions but some of the most exciting do span into the physical world as well – they are phygital.

- Combining AI from different fields: gaming technology is leading the way in many aspects of AI. How many of these techniques can be applied in your business? How many can improve your employees' experience?

These points hint at innovation approaches, they do not suggest an innovation that will improve the customer proposition or go to meet an unrecognised need. The following sections give some ideas that can be immediately put to use in organisations today but should be read in combination with the sections that cover how AI is being applied to the creative industries and abstract thinking.

Generative AI and ideation

You need ideas to innovate and there is nothing better than a logical thinking virtual assistant to help you. Enter generative AI solutions such as ChatGPT-4o that can help you elaborate on your idea and flesh it out by adding more details to it. Box 4.1 shows how ChatGPT-4o assisted me with my idea to create a service to help elderly people who do not have access to technology to handle their day-to-day needs, such as banking, booking appointments, paying for parking, shopping and so on, in an increasingly digital world where paper money and coins are more or less obsolete.

While I knew that such a service is needed from my personal experience of caring for my elderly mother, I had no idea as to how it might work. ChatGPT-4o amazed me by its ability to suggest various solutions that when combined would provide a comprehensive service. It self-prompted to take my idea from start to finish as a proposition, and then, on my prompt, it created an image of the proposed solution to make my new service a reality.

Because of its self-prompting, ChatGPT-4o was behaving like agentic AI, in my opinion. Agentic AI is a separate field from generative AI but generative AI can be agentic in some contexts, for example when content creation is needed. Agentic AI is an emerging field of autonomous AI, like autonomous vehicles, that is designed to do specific things entirely by itself. This could be automation of a process from end-to-end including any decision-making autonomously. Examples of agentic AI include recruitment robots that are instructed to find candidates with certain qualifications and experience. They meticulously scan CVs to produce a shortlist based on those requirements without further human intervention.

In the example below, ChatGPT-4o seemed to me to behave like an innovation agentic AI. Its self-prompting took the ideation from concept to solution with only two prompts from me; the initial question that I put to it and the image creation of the service at the end. It did not come up with risks and challenges but it would have done had I prompted it. Overall, the proposition was good enough to get me started had I been serious about the business idea.

My conversation with ChatGPT-4o and how it fleshed out my business idea and then produced images of what it had proposed is described in Box 4.1.

BOX 4.1 HOW ChatGPT-4o ASSISTED MY IDEA TO CREATE A SERVICE TO HELP ELDERLY PEOPLE WHO DO NOT HAVE ACCESS TO TECHNOLOGY TO HANDLE THEIR DAY-TO-DAY NEEDS

Me: Can you help me create a product that helps elderly folks, who have no access to the web, deal with digital services?

ChatGPT-4o:

Concept: DigiHelp - Bridging the Digital Divide for Elderly Folks

Product Name: DigiHelp

Tagline: Empowering the Elderly with Digital Assistance

Overview:

DigiHelp is a service designed to help elderly individuals who lack access to the web and digital devices. This product combines personalised, human-assisted services with simple, accessible technologies to bridge the digital divide and ensure that elderly people can efficiently manage their digital services and needs.

Key Features:

- Human-Assisted Hotline:
  - 24/7 Support: A toll-free hotline staffed by trained agents who can assist with a wide range of digital services.
  - Personalised Assistance: Agents can handle tasks like booking medical appointments, managing utility bills, or ordering groceries online on behalf of the user.
  - Trusted Contacts: Users can designate trusted family members or friends to communicate with the hotline on their behalf.

- Voice-Activated Assistance Device:
  - Easy Set-Up: A plug-and-play device that connects to the user's phone line, allowing them to interact with digital services through voice commands.
  - Voice Commands: Simple, natural language commands to request services, information, or connect with the hotline.
  - Emergency Features: One-touch emergency assistance that connects to the hotline or designated contacts.
- Physical Mail Integration:
  - Mail-In Requests: Users can send written requests or bills to a central processing centre where agents digitise and handle them.
  - Regular Updates: Periodic mailed summaries of the user's digital activities and status updates.
- Local Community Centres:
  - In-Person Support: Partnerships with local community centres or libraries where trained staff can assist elderly individuals with digital services.
  - Workshops and Training: Regular workshops to educate elderly individuals on basic digital literacy and the use of the DigiHelp services.
- Mobile App for Caregivers:
  - Remote Monitoring: Family members or caregivers can use the app to monitor the services and requests made on behalf of the elderly individual.
  - Notifications and Alerts: Real-time notifications for any urgent issues or completed tasks.
  - Communication Hub: Facilitates communication between the elderly individual, their family, and DigiHelp agents.

Implementation Plan:

- Market Research and Validation:
  - Conduct surveys and focus groups with elderly individuals and their families to understand their needs and preferences.
  - Collaborate with senior living communities and organisations to validate the concept.
- Partnership Development:
  - Partner with telecommunications companies to provide the voice-activated assistance device.
  - Establish collaborations with local community centres and libraries for in-person support.

- Technology Development:
  - Develop the voice-activated assistance device with a focus on ease of use and reliability.
  - Create the back-end systems for the hotline and mail-in request processing.
  - Develop the caregiver mobile app with secure access and user-friendly features.
- Pilot Programme:
  - Launch a pilot programme in select cities or regions to test the service and gather feedback.
  - Adjust and refine the service based on user experiences and feedback.
- Marketing and Outreach:
  - Develop marketing materials targeting elderly individuals and their families through traditional media, community events, and partnerships with senior organisations.
  - Utilise testimonials and case studies from the pilot programme to showcase the benefits of DigiHelp.
- Full-Scale Launch:
  - Roll out DigiHelp nationally with a robust support infrastructure.
  - Continuously monitor and improve the service based on user feedback and technological advancements.

Benefits:

- Makes digital services accessible to elderly individuals without requiring them to navigate complex technologies.
- Peace of Mind: Provides family members and caregivers with assurance that their loved ones are supported.
- Independence: Empowers elderly individuals to manage their daily needs without relying solely on others.
- Community Engagement: Strengthens community ties by involving local centres and volunteers in the support network.

DigiHelp aims to bridge the digital divide for elderly individuals, ensuring they can enjoy the benefits of digital services without the associated challenges. By combining human assistance with accessible technology, DigiHelp provides a comprehensive solution to enhance the quality of life for the elderly.

Me: What would the product look like?

ChatGPT-4o

Visual Concept for DigiHelp

1. Voice-Activated Assistance Device:

   - Design: Compact, simple, and user-friendly.

   - Appearance: A small, sleek, rectangular device with large, clearly labelled buttons and a built-in microphone and speaker.

   - Features:

     - Large Buttons: Clearly labelled for common functions like 'Call Hotline,' 'Request Service,' and 'Emergency.'

     - Display Screen: Small LED screen for displaying simple messages or confirmations.

     - Voice Activation: Can be activated through simple voice commands like 'DigiHelp, call support' or 'DigiHelp, order groceries.'

   - Image Prompt: A sleek, rectangular voice-activated assistance device with large, clearly labelled buttons for 'Call Hotline,' 'Request Service,' and 'Emergency.' It features a small LED display and built-in microphone and speaker.

2. Human-Assisted Hotline Interface:

   - Design: Professional and reassuring, reflecting a welcoming and supportive atmosphere.

   - Appearance: Call centre with friendly, trained agents, equipped with headsets and computer terminals displaying user profiles and requests.

   - Image Prompt: A modern call centre with friendly, trained agents wearing headsets, using computer terminals displaying user profiles and requests.

3. Physical Mail Integration:

   - Design: A centralised mail processing centre.

   - Appearance: Staff sorting through physical mail, scanning documents, and inputting data into digital systems.

   - Image Prompt: A centralised mail processing centre with staff sorting and scanning physical mail, converting it into digital data.

4. Local Community Centre Kiosks:

   - Design: Accessible kiosks or help desks located in community centres or libraries.

   - Appearance: Bright, inviting kiosks with touch screens and friendly staff ready to assist.

   - Image Prompt: Bright, inviting kiosks in a community centre with touch screens and friendly staff assisting elderly individuals.

5. Mobile App for Caregivers:

- Design: Intuitive and user-friendly, with a focus on clear information and ease of use.

- Appearance: A clean, modern interface showing notifications, task status, and options for remote monitoring.

- Image Prompt: A clean, modern mobile app interface showing notifications, task status, and options for remote monitoring, designed for caregivers.

Final Composite Image Concept:

A collage featuring:

- The sleek voice-activated assistance device with large buttons and an LED screen.

- A friendly call centre with agents wearing headsets.

- A mail processing centre with staff sorting mail.

- Inviting kiosks at a community centre with touch screens.

- A modern mobile app interface for caregivers.

Image Prompt for Composite:

- A collage featuring a sleek voice-activated assistance device with large, clearly labelled buttons and an LED screen; a friendly call centre with agents wearing headsets; a centralised mail processing centre with staff sorting mail; inviting kiosks at a community centre with touch screens and friendly staff; and a modern mobile app interface for caregivers showing notifications and task status.

This image has been generated by AI.

Business models

While AI might boost your product or service ideation to help with innovation, it might also boost your ideas for new business models. There are many examples of innovative and disruptive business models. Airbnb, Rightmove, Peloton and Uber are all good mainstream examples. Many of these organisations were able to disrupt existing industries because of the advent of the World Wide Web in conjunction with smartphones. In fact, there are now literally thousands of companies that have introduced a new business model into their own sectors – and that change has been made possible by new communications technology.

It is generally accepted that these new models were enabled by a combination of the following factors, highlighted many years ago by Lee in his 2001 paper *An Analytical Framework for Evaluating E-commerce Business Models and Strategies* (Lee, 2001):

- reduction in transaction costs;
- transfer of risk;
- changing trust balance;
- untapped capacity;
- disintermediation;
- transparency;
- real-world monitoring through the IoT.

When Lee outlined the seven points in his paper in 2001 he could see these factors would impact business models. However, it wasn't until many years later that the disruptive businesses mentioned above emerged.

One of the points that I make in this book is that the technology shift due to AI is every bit as disruptive, if not more, as the web and smartphones and arguably speeds up the pace of disruption.

Here, I look at how AI adds a huge step change into the factors that disrupt business models with some examples that are already emerging. Many new models will emerge, but from the evidence already available there are at least four types of models that are actively enabled by AI:

- micro outsourcing;
- changing commercial boundaries;
- changing physical boundaries;
- high-value technical advances.

I look at each of these models in turn and give examples of organisations that are exploiting the change.

Micro outsourcing

Transaction costs, untapped capacity, reduction in production costs: these three factors led to the viability of externalising specialised but small-volume services. Because of the smaller volumes than are normally associated with outsourcing this is sometimes called micro outsourcing. AI will accelerate this trend because some types of micro outsourcing can be made much more efficient, for example by automating narrow services that are supplied to many organisations.

An example is AI music generating tools. They use AI to generate music, for example soundtracks for videos. Providing these services at a feasible cost has been difficult in the past, but now AI can be used to both understand the brief, in this case the type and style of music overlay, say, for a corporate video, and then produce the soundtrack. This is a good example of a service that is quite difficult to source in small volumes for a typical business, but can be supplied to multiple organisations at a fraction of the price of using an internal team.

Extending the function of an intelligent home speaker or assistant to take account of the sound emitted by your home's smoke alarm or the sound of breaking glass is another example. This is where specialist monitoring equipment and services such as alarm systems are being disrupted by not only reduced transaction costs, but also replacement of relatively low-volume parts by a general device (the smart speaker), thereby greatly reducing the cost of production.

The ability to reduce the risk or cost of a particular process due to the investment in AI is evidenced by companies that offer robots for harvesting fruit. Typically, the mechanism for picking fruit and the AI that controls it are closely integrated. The companies can contain the risk of using the machine in a glasshouse setting and reduce the cost of the process of picking and placing the fruit in punnets. They offer to outsource this process for farmers, not by providing the equipment but by outsourcing the 'fruit-to-punnet' process.

A further example emerges from 3D printing. Although not an AI technology in its own right, there are now services that allow you to upload a 2D photograph. AI is then applied to 'guess' the 3D shape of the subject from the hints in the 2D image. Depending on the level of skill needed to control and optimise the 3D rendering, it may be that this work is completed by a 3D printing shop, or completely in-sourced because it is the best way to get from a photograph to a physical prototype through your own 3D printing equipment. This is using technology powered by AI to create new services and commercial models – something that was not easy to do before its widespread use. Although these services are mostly based on information with some impact on the physical world, it is reasonable to expect this balance to change as more general purpose intelligent assistants become available.

Changing commercial boundaries

Almost every commercial boundary between a company and its stakeholders – customers, suppliers, regulators – has been challenged by the disruptive models of the last 20 years, and I would argue that the AI revolution will increase the pace of that disruption in the future.

Between customers and companies it seems likely that customers will demand a better service before they commit to a purchase or a brand. Competitors will find ways to provide attractive services at very low cost using AI. These services may require a 'freemium' offer as we see in the software industry when a product or service is offered without charge for a period of time to allow customers to try the product before paying for it.

Continuing the thoughts about micro outsourcing, the relationship with suppliers will change in a similar way. On the other hand, the efficiency gained through your deployment of AI might mean that it is more beneficial to bring a service that has been outsourced in-house.

The services that are currently outsourced will be candidates for in-sourcing. There is no point in paying for a large off-shore contact centre when an automated customer interface can handle the service requests better and at a reduced cost.

Changing physical boundaries
As AI impacts the physical world, the current physical boundaries around an organisation will be challenged. Sometimes it will continue to make sense to manufacture in large factories. In other cases manufacturing close to the demand will become feasible and be more efficient. If we treat house building as a form of manufacturing, we have a great example of changing physical boundaries. There are many projects around the world (CyBe, Icon) which show that 3D printing can be applied to domestic house building and industrial construction projects. Proponents of these projects say that there are three advantages:

- A common design can be used for many implementations of the same building.

- A variety of expensive low-volume parts can be replaced with standard blocks or a specific type of fluid concrete that can be built up in layers.

- Most of the build is mechanised and the results matched back to the specification.

The economics of construction can be changed dramatically using these three measures. It has been hundreds of years since the cost of manufacture for transportable goods was minimised by using factories that delivered at scale, but the model could not be applied to construction. In this case, 3D printing can deliver some of those efficiency advantages without being constrained by factory walls.

Equally, organisations will be able to provide a service where the demand is needed, away from their main or regional offices. An example is how some local authorities, due to financial constraints, are using their libraries, community centres or job centres to provide online services to clients that might not have access to the internet at home. The councils provide kiosks equipped with PCs to allow customers to access services online. The customers can ask questions about their services that are then answered automatically by a chatbot and, if necessary, passed to an expert, who might be available in person at that location or working remotely. In this way, the customer gets a better service at a location that is convenient for them while the council makes maximum use of its expert resources wherever they are located. This was particularly useful during the COVID-19 pandemic when customers were able to pop in to their nearest facility to access services online and the council's experts were able to continue to offer help and advice while working in their preferred work locations, with services partially automated or augmented by chatbots.

High-value technical advances

The most disruptive models will be those with a value proposition that is a leap in the eyes of the customer. Typically these will be the large-scale moon-shot plays and there will probably be a relatively small number of organisations that end up with commercially transformative products. We know that the likes of self-driving cars, user interfaces for computers and personal service platforms will be continually enhanced. For example, already, we are seeing generative AI powering increased personalisation of services for customers. There is talk of customers getting their own version of virtual assistants when they log in to a provider's website. The virtual assistant powered by generative AI will be able to converse with the customer in the context of the services or products that they obtain from the provider and use their past interactions to help and advise them, or go further and actually handle their query, for example offer personal shopper services. The service could be provided by a personal shopper robot provider on a micro outsourcing basis to the business in question.

Such transformative products and services enabled by advances in AI will catch the headlines, and a small number of organisations will probably transform the way we live using applications of AI that may not have even been imagined yet. However, the bigger effect on our lives will come from how AI impacts almost every organisation. To visualise this, the following sections describe innovation within a corporate context – markets, processes, products – and then lead on to the fascinating area of AI in the creative industries.

Markets

Financial markets may be the first place that the implications of AI become clear. The rise and rise of algorithmic trading in the financial markets is an interesting indicator. As Purba Mukerji (2019) observes, algorithmic trading started as a minor activity in the 1990s but recently accounted for 60 to 75 per cent of trades in US, European and major Asian capital markets (Groette, 2024). The algorithms have changed over this period of time, and the degree of intelligence has increased with every advancing year. It is fair to conclude that in the most competitive of markets, large organisations are putting their trust in these algorithms to judge price and timing better than skilled traders. So if AI can make such a big impact on financial markets, how will it affect other markets?

Maybe it is reasonable to expect that if capital markets provide the environment for the earliest adoption of technologies then retail financial markets are a close second. The rise of robo-advisors is an interesting example. These systems are relatively simple, and regulation, thankfully, means they cannot be unconstrained. Nonetheless, the types of predictive personal shopper that may be a feature of other retail markets may make more of an appearance in financial markets in the future too.

Any market where decisions by market actors can be improved with more transparent information or better predictions can be disrupted, such as the travel or retail industries where information about prices and offers is widely available. When you consider innovation in the market that your organisation operates in, price discovery, better prediction of supply and demand, and difficult to anticipate disruption are factors to consider.

Processes

This book has many examples of processes that are totally changed through AI: application processes, fulfilment processes, customer service processes and so on. One example that is apt to discuss in this context is AI's role in process innovation. I believe the following examples illustrate this point well.

A contact centre operator achieved major benefits rapidly from application of AI in process optimisation. All processes involve steps sequenced in time. In large organisations with many people, these process steps can vary as staff adopt different practices over time. To understand the level of variations in what should be standardised processes, the contact centre operator uses a task mining tool to discover exactly what the processes are and how long each step takes. It then uses the information to drive process improvements, firstly through a top-down approach that takes best practice and codifies it for everyone, using technology to automate some steps in the target group of processes, and, secondly, through bottom–up process improvement with training, measurement and successive refinement. Without the AI tool it would be infeasible to capture, collect and analyse all the process-related information in a way that shows the patterns and the opportunities for improvement and process modernisation.

Calderdale Council provides another example in the case study in Chapter 7. Here the business driver was to increase the levels of self-service, a strategy that delivered more benefits than expected because of the COVID-19 pandemic that increased demand for online services. The AI front-end that was added to the council's website enabled the customer to start a conversation that allowed the right expert or advisor to be consulted should it be necessary. The conversational interface answered questions first and fully whenever possible but if the case needed to be handled by an expert the routing and summary information meant the right advisor was brought into the conversation with the history of the case at least partly provided to them.

I believe that it is possible to characterise the impact of AI on process innovation as follows:

- process discovery or process or task mining to identify the optimisation needed;
- incremental automation (e.g. image and voice processing);
- outsourcing replacement (e.g. music for videos);
- process analytics (virtual assistants, predictive answers);
- physical process changes (e.g. pothole filling, simple deliveries, social care service platforms);
- self-mending processes (automated exception handling).

Examples of each of these types of process innovation are provided in this book and can be translated into many other commercial and public sector settings.

Products and services

Innovative AI products are being invented every day. From the 'Generating ideas' section at the start of this chapter, these products can be classified as either a moon-shot technology leap or an AI increment on existing proven products. In this section I concentrate on the second category, because it is more relevant to the majority of organisations.

To enhance your product, you can consider using one of the areas where AI has proven itself in a commercial setting:

- NLP;
- analysis and prediction;
- image recognition and classification;
- generative AI for conversational interfaces, synthetic data generation for AI product development, or adding features such as the ability to generate reports from data or interpret the data and summarise the findings;
- where relevant using generative AI to add features to generate new content and digital assets such as music, videos and artwork;
- process optimisation and exception handling;
- extensions to the physical environment;
- gaming technology.

You may then be able to use AI with existing technology that you have already deployed or apply it in a different way to gain improvements. The following section gives several examples and shows how selecting complementary solutions can be effective.

AI in combination with other solutions

In many business settings the ideas with the best returns will probably be based on AI in combination with other technologies. With this notion in mind, here is a list of combinations of technologies that are getting traction in projects and organisations around the world.

AI in the physical world

Vacuum cleaners, lawn mowers and pool cleaners have been automated for some time with increasing intelligence built in. The universal butler is still some way off. What will be the next 'killer app' in the physical robot world? In this section I explore a few ideas that hint at what is to come.

The need for additional resources in adult social care is well documented. Kind, empathetic people are needed but there are not enough of them. If time-consuming repetitive tasks can be taken off their work schedule then they have more time to provide empathy and comfort. In Japan this idea is better accepted than in many other cultures; they have used service robots for helping rather than replacing caring human beings. Their approach broadly is to use the service robots to do the fetching, carrying and other routine tasks to leave the carers to spend more time with people.

> Closer to home here in the UK, one example of the kinds of project that are advancing applications of AI in social care is Care at Home using Intelligent Robotic Omni-function Nodes (CHIRON) (CHIRON, 2018). This was a project funded by Innovate UK, to design care robotics that ensure dignity, independence and choice. It ran from 2016 to 2018 and resulted in a prototype modular robotic system called JUVA, that was not one robot but a set of modular intelligent solutions, positioned in different places around the home to help people with tasks throughout the day.

Service robots for local deliveries are well established with many small and large area trials. Service robots for domestic use are less well advanced.

It is reasonable to extrapolate the use of digital assistants with existing, though not widely used, service robots. Maybe starting with just monitoring, then information provision, such as reminders for medication with light-touch monitoring, then progressively going phygital with more useful physical assistance.

Digital prototyping is used to visualise new products, buildings and landscapes. For some types of products, and even buildings, once they can be visualised they can be built using advances in 3D printing.

Innovation in these areas will continue apace because they are the subject of mainstream research investment. In the meantime, there will be incremental innovation by combining existing technologies with AI.

AI and process automation
IA and IPA including intelligent document processing have been the route to large-scale savings in many organisations. There is an increasing role for more AI to combine with these technologies.

Opportunities exist with software solutions today to capture information about a process and re-engineer it, improve it through conversational interfaces, embedded AI within data entry forms and then a combination of AI with RPA technologies or application programming interfaces (APIs). Chapter 5 discusses many technologies that enable process automation.

Just by examining the case studies in this book it is easy to see how a business process can be re-engineered. The high-cost areas of the process can then be further automated using NLP and conversational interfaces and continually improving exception handling. The continually improving exception handling evolves into an adaptive process. If an exception occurs more than 10 per cent of the time then it is generally accepted that it is a path through the process and not an exception. A common area in which these exceptions occur is the integration between systems. AI has a specific role in these technologies to change the task from 'transfer this record that represents a service request into back office system A' to 'a customer has reported a potential fault with these characteristics'. The AI then learns how that situation should be represented in the back office system and the limitations of the import mechanism, be it through an API, RPA engine or batch record imports. The result would be a set of processes that are continually evolving to engineer out exceptions with the AI learning from the process.

AI and the Internet of Things

For many business processes there is an input or output that impacts the direct physical world. Continuing the example from the previous section, which discussed aspects of a fault handling process, the fault could have been directly reported by a device in the field. This is an example of the IoT. It may also be that manufacturers choose to make their error displays such that an image contains all the information needed to process the fault. The image is forwarded by the customer or person who inspects the machine and it is recognised and parsed by AI to initiate the process of resolving the fault.

Other processes would be initiated by physical devices, for example when an alarm goes off to indicate a break in a part of a physical intrusion detection system. Another example is reactive and planned maintenance for connected plant and machinery, when automated testing of machinery is activated based on a daily schedule at the end of the day. In the home, these processes are likely to be oriented around a small number of trusted devices, making those devices more important.

AI and augmented desktops

For many typical office-based roles, including knowledge workers, designers, sales agents and customer service agents, there are AI helpers that work with the combination of systems that are already in use and assist the employee. Examples are best answers, next best action recommendation engines and cross-sell and up-sell recommendation engines. Some of these systems are proprietary and part of, for example, customer relationship management systems. More recently, Microsoft and Google have added generative AI helpers to their personal productivity suites where users can get help with a variety of things including text generation, text editing and rewriting, synthesising information from chats in collaboration workspaces, creative content generation like a catchy slogan, and code writing.

AI and conversational forms

Organisations ask customers to complete complex online forms. Unfortunately the more complex the form, the more likely a customer is to make a mistake. For example, in claims for Child and Working Tax Credits in the UK, errors account for over 4 per cent overpayment (HM Revenue and Customs, 2020), which represents more than £1 billion per year. To enhance accuracy a conversational interface can help, particularly if there is specialist language or terms involved.

AI and application development platforms

Organisations that create application development tools are actively introducing AI into their products. Although it is not the focus of this book, which is aimed at business use of AI rather than its technical uses, it is interesting to see how this field is developing because it shows some of the future paths that will influence the use of AI in business:

- AI-created systems: these systems are created from the ground up starting with requirements through design, test and deployment and ongoing improvements. Currently this approach is only feasible for relatively simple systems such as websites with well-characterised functionality. There are already numerous AI-powered tools that assist people in both the design and creation of websites.

AI is revolutionising the field. Tools like Adobe Sensei and Wix ADI (Artificial Design Intelligence) can analyse user preferences and generate aesthetically pleasing website layouts and more. These AI solutions can automatically adjust design elements, optimise user experience, and even personalise content. Generative AI, such as ChatGPT, is capable of producing program code as well. In fact, many tools aid developers in various aspects of their work including creating code snippets. Examples include auto-complete tools like Kite for Python. Another notable example is GitHub Copilot, which leverages AI to help developers write code more efficiently by suggesting lines, or even entire functions, as they type.

- There are also tools that attempt to automatically fix code that is causing errors to be reported, such as DrRepair (https://worksheets.codalab.org/worksheets/0x01 838644724a433c932bef4cb5c42fbd).

As these tools rapidly develop and converge it is reasonable to extrapolate a bit further and see that the process of specification will become streamlined through a conversation or dialogue that introduces enough visual and time-based elements to be able to assemble more complex systems. A machine-generated specification producing the working product is within the future capabilities of many current platforms.

AI in games platforms and product innovation
Games creators are constantly pushing the boundaries of current technology and that includes AI. Many would argue that the behaviour of so-called non-player characters (NPCs) is a stringent test for AI in other applications. There is a clear crossover between that aspect of games technology and the virtual assistant toolkits that are currently mainstream in the corporate world. There are companies that already target this point of need, combining the AI of a chatbot with the avatar rendering of a games engine (example: www.pinscreen.com/avatar-neo-creator-app).

Games environments are also being used to provide test-beds for AI of different types. A paper by DeepMind called 'Using Unity to help solve intelligence' (DeepMind, 2020) describes a joint initiative with the widely used Unity gaming platform. A toolkit called ML-Agents within Unity allows NPCs to be trained rather than scripted or coded. That in turn puts an emphasis on making the gaming environment a sufficient simulation to train the avatar. This has a parallel with the way, for example, that autonomous car makers are using simulation environments to ensure that their AI is well trained before it sees a test track.

So the worlds of video games and corporate IT are already merging and the underlying technology is already in place. The right customer experience will combine with cultural acceptance and business need to provide disruptive products in this area.

AI and enterprise resource planning
Vendors of ERP solutions, such as Oracle and SAP, are adding more AI capabilities to their products. This is important because ERP software is very widely adopted across industries. Consequently, there is more and more AI being deployed across organisations. ERP systems can be broad, in terms of both the business functions used and adoption within an organisation. There will be many potential uses of AI.

For the modules that are used by a large number of occasional users (e.g. expenses, employee benefits, ad hoc procurement) then conversational interfaces either using text or voice will most likely be of benefit.

Of more profound impact will be the use of AI to reduce the number of process-related exceptions or to automatically handle exceptions when they do arise. Invoice and order exceptions in large organisations can easily run at 10 to 20 per cent. Reducing this rate both reduces cost and probably improves overall data quality. It is that data quality which leads to possibly the most important role of AI in ERP and that is to use the very rich data resources to build better predictions and to identify anomalies in the data that tend to get masked using standard aggregation techniques.

AI and IT service delivery

Due to its technical nature, IT service delivery has been an early adopter of AI. In fact, the very specialised field of intrusion detection and monitoring for cybersecurity was one of the earliest areas to use AI to try to spot unusual patterns of use. There are many other uses of AI within IT service delivery, for example detecting potential system failures from past performance or proactively and automatically managing infrastructure to avoid computing performance issues.

In the context of innovation, the degree to which AI is used in IT infrastructure management is increasing and there is even talk of self-aware infrastructures that effectively look after themselves through means such as pattern matching, root cause analysis, event correlation and forecasting as part of managing operations. This is often referred to as AI for IT operations or AIOps for short. Examples include monitoring demand for services and spinning up or decommissioning servers in the cloud as needed, or preventing and countering cyberattacks.

AI AND CREATIVITY

In this book I concentrate on the business applications of AI and so this short sortie into the world of the creative arts is just to complement the use of AI in other areas. I present a few examples that show how AI can enhance or change the process of creating paintings and music. Then I briefly discuss the application of AI to abstract reasoning.

Painting and imagery

AI image creation is not new. In fact, an early milestone in AI-generated imagery was an image printed on canvas and titled *Edmond de Belamy*. It captured the headlines in 2018. This is shown in Figure 4.1.

In the image, the subject is a man who can only just be made out. The image was created by a group of French students in an art collective called Obvious, using generative adversarial networks (GANs). GANs are a type of machine learning framework where two neural networks, a generator and a discriminator, compete against each other in a zero-sum game. The generator creates new data instances, while the discriminator evaluates their authenticity. This adversarial training process pushes both networks to improve, ultimately resulting in the generator producing highly realistic, synthetic data that can fool the discriminator. In this example of use of a GAN, the portrait was called *Edmond de Belamy*, a play on the name of Ian Goodfellow, the creator of GANs.

Figure 4.1 A 2018 AI-generated portrait titled *Edmond de Belamy* (Source: Wikipedia)

If you ask AI to produce an image today you get a much more detailed picture. An example of one production is shown in Figure 4.2. The figure clearly shows advances that have been made in AI since *Edmond de Belamy* was created in 2018.

Figure 4.2 A 2024 portrait of a man in 18th-century European style produced by DALL-E through a ChatGPT-4o prompt: 'Can you generate an image of a man in 18th-century European style?'

Generative AI can also produce videos. There are already many technology vendors that offer text to video generation. The big generative AI players, namely Google and OpenAI, have their own offerings called Veo and Sora respectively.

For image and video generation, diffusion models are used to create data. Diffusion models are a class of generative models that create realistic samples by simulating a diffusion process. This involves gradually adding random noise to data and then reversing the process to remove the noise, thereby generating new data that resembles the original dataset.

Of more direct applicability for business is the ability to take a sketch and turn it into an artist's impression of, say, a building. Furthermore, the image can then be given the artistic style that you want. Although most systems of this kind are in their early prototype stage, it is clear that the ability to turn a rough sketch into an image and then a design is not far away.

Music

Creating music has been a field of AI for several decades. There are various AI-powered music producing sites like Aitubo and Media.io. Their web-based facilities provide ways to create music, for example for videos, matching the style and mood of the music to the video. This is an otherwise awkward facility to create without specialist skills so is a use of creative AI that immediately applies to business. Other providers include Google and its Magenta offering for AI-generated music.

There are many more AI music composers that range from the simple to those that require professional music knowledge and are designed to enhance the skills of accomplished composers. For those with a particular interest in this field there is an annual AI song contest (www.aisongcontest.com/) during which teams compete for the best composition. Most AI competitions are taken very seriously but this one is a bit more light-hearted.

Abstract problem solving

Finally in this section I briefly discuss how AI is moving into abstract problem solving. That is, away from closed questions like 'is this an image of a cat?' to the types of problems with a desired answer but no clear way of structuring the path to the result. An example might be, 'When should I launch product A?' There is no right answer, but neural networks can be used to try to infer a way of getting to an answer and then provide an explanation of their method. Generative AI is already capable of handling these types of questions to some degree.

This is a research field, but recent developments where AI has excelled at winning board games like Go show that progress is being made. In addition, AI has shown that it can deal with complex mathematical problems. AI-powered abstract problem solving may apply to business very soon with the level of effort that is being applied. The architecture in a paper by a team at DeepMind, *Measuring abstract reasoning in neural networks* (Lillicrap, 2018), shows one approach that can be applied directly.

In this example a specific class of abstract problem was chosen. The neural networks were set up to try to infer the way that a pattern was derived from other patterns. There

Figure 4.3 The AI fountain from which springs the potential for augmented human work in the digital and physical worlds, and smarter machines (Source: Background photo of fountains by Jaël Vallée on Unsplash)

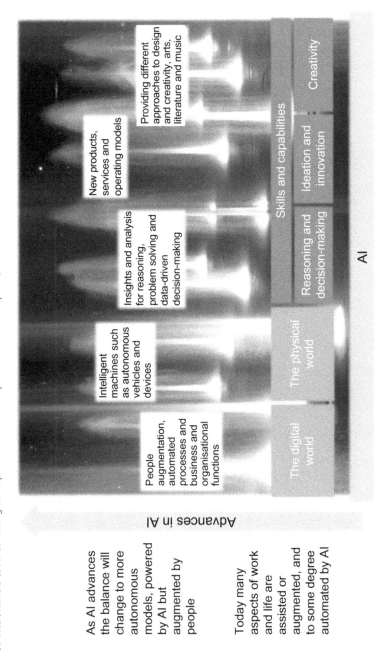

was always a way of deriving the answer in these examples and although the paper starts with a reference to one of Einstein's thought experiments, it is not clear how the technique could be generalised that far. But it is clear how it could answer, 'Is there a best time to launch product A?' or even, given past history, 'Should I launch product A or C next?'

Neural networks that can provide directly commercially useful abstract thinking are starting to appear. We are set for a significant leap forward in decision-support systems.

THE AI FOUNTAIN

So far I have covered AI for innovation and how it can go across intersections of the digital and physical worlds, in business as well as arts and creativity. In the next chapter I cover AI for efficiency.

To bring all the threads in this chapter together, I have created a visualisation of AI as a fountain from which springs the potential for enhanced human work in the digital and physical worlds, and smarter machines. It will also help with skills and capabilities, for example providing data for reasoning and decision-making, and different approaches to design and innovation, as well as creativity. AI is already augmenting some human work and activity, and, as it advances, it will be enabling autonomic systems that in time will lead to autonomous enterprises. This is where humans will augment AI to ensure the quality of its operations, its governance and ethical, human-centric behaviour.

These ideas are captured in Figure 4.3.

SUMMARY

In this chapter I examined the role of AI in business innovation. I started by looking at applications of AI within the process of innovation by using it to discover new customer demand and the generation of new ideas. Then, using a generally accepted definition of innovation in business, I explored how AI can help with ideation for innovation with an example produced by ChatGPT. I then explored the role of AI in innovation in business models, markets, products and services.

To provide as many specific examples as possible, I looked at combinations of AI with other technologies. These combinations are likely to contribute the most immediate gains in many organisations. In particular, I looked at combining a common use of AI, such as NLP, or generative AI or image classification, with existing technologies. The availability of relatively mature toolkits in some of the more established AI fields means that these projects that combine technologies can be implemented relatively simply.

The need to focus on the practical and achievable should not detract from some of the uses of AI that are more far-reaching. Although I only touch briefly on the use of AI in art and music, the very fact that there are now practical products and services being launched in that field is profound. Even more fundamental is the use of AI for abstract problem solving.

If the regulators stay ahead of the technical developments, and the ethical considerations raised by AI are well and truly taken in hand, then the increasing power and breadth of the technology can help with some of society's most intractable issues.

In a corporate context, there are some ideas in this chapter that should at least contribute to the debate in many organisations. Each idea or solution put forward includes an example that shows how the technology is being used in real life. How radical you want to be in your organisation will be dictated by your own environment, but I hope there are some ideas here you can build on.

Finally, I introduced the AI fountain out of which springs many new developments that will give us a variety of capabilities – from AI assistance and augmentation to autonomic systems that we will use and augment to ensure their relevance and human-centric operation and behaviour.

To relate all of this back to autonomous enterprises, many early adopters of AI in business will have a huge advantage over others simply because of the data that they will accumulate from their intelligent digital transactions. The data can be mined to identify patterns that point to opportunities for innovation. Therefore, I fully expect autonomous enterprises to also be very innovative. More to come on this in Chapter 10.

5   AI FOR EFFICIENCY

In this chapter I discuss uses of AI to boost business efficiency, an objective that leading organisations strive for as part of ambitious continuous improvement programmes that increasingly include automating processes. These in turn are leading to the evolution of organisations into autonomous enterprises where the bulk of high-volume, repetitive and transactional work as well as many customer interactions and decision-making tasks will be done by machines. In turn, humans will only get involved in supervision of the work, guiding the software robots and handling exceptions or in customer interactions where empathy is needed. They will continue to develop, maintain and supervise the automations.

Increasing efficiency year-on-year is a major driver for investment in technology and for many projects that enterprises undertake. Much of the effort has been focused on improving the front line of operations where interactions with customers happen, as well as line of business and administrative processes. In recent years employee engagement has also come into sharper focus, rising as an enterprise priority. This is driven by a shortage of skills and the costs of hiring.

Applications of intelligent technology will help by augmenting human workers, enabling them to work faster and better while reducing their repetitive and uninteresting workload. For example, AI can help contact centre agents by delivering information to them in real time, in the context of the conversation that they are having with customers, to help them answer questions faster and better, or walk them through the next steps of a complicated process. This is what I call human augmentation, where technology helps staff with their daily tasks, to increase productivity, job satisfaction levels and consequently reducing staff attrition and costs of hiring and skills development. Generative AI is already proving to be one of the most useful types of AI for everyday knowledge work with its conversational ability to answer questions and generate content on demand, among other things.

AI for process automation can learn to augment humans in different ways, for example by following the work of subject matter experts and learning how they deal with processes and exceptions. It can analyse data about interactions, such as how calls were handled on similar subjects in the past, or use a custom-built knowledge base.

AI can significantly aid enterprises in various ways as they strive for greater efficiency. In this chapter, I first provide a few examples of AI for efficiency in settings other than office-based business processes. Then, I focus on enablers of the autonomous enterprise and its automated business functions. I delve into a group of technologies that can deliver efficiency in the context of enterprise business processes and knowledge work automation.

BRINGING AI FOR EFFICIENCY TO LIFE

The case studies in Chapters 6 to 9 provide real life examples of AI enabling process efficiency. These are from a diverse group of organisations that vary in size and nature of work. There are many other examples too and I cover a number of them in the following sections.

AI to improve decision-making

AI can be used to improve decision-making. The ability to make decisions based on hard facts is always important but particularly so in times of uncertainty and increased business complexity. A prime example during the pandemic, when workforce illness disrupted supply chains, was the critical need to maintain the flow of essential supplies. Some organisations were using advanced analytics powered by machine learning to identify where in their vast network of warehouses they had surplus supplies. These could then be diverted to where there was a shortage to assure business continuity in the affected locations. The same capabilities can be used at other times of crisis and when natural disasters impact the supply chain.

Another example is AI helping physicians make better decisions by analysing the results of X-rays and computerised tomography (CT) scans, as described in the case study in Chapter 8 on improving stroke care at the Royal Berkshire NHS Foundation Trust (RBFT). The software deployed at RBFT helps emergency doctors to better diagnose the damage caused by stroke. This, combined with other steps to make the care process more efficient, is improving overall patient outcomes, particularly for those who present out of hours when emergency doctors may not be able to reach specialists to consult nor have experienced radiologists available to diagnose the extent of the damage shown in the scans. The technology not only identifies the likely locations of brain clots shown by the scan, it also allows the images to be quickly shared with specialists who are not on site, on their mobiles or other hand-held devices. This enables emergency doctors to consult the specialists remotely and decide the best course of treatment and referrals for the patient. The investment in AI has resulted in patients receiving the appropriate treatment faster and has significantly improved the chances of them returning to normal life after their strokes.

Another example of AI in decision support is that covered in Chapter 9 – Wärtsilä's use of an intelligent configure price quote (CPQ) solution that helps their sales consultants to correctly configure complex power generation or ship engines to price and quote for. It also helps them to understand the impact of changing components and parts or an updated design on the chosen configuration and the pricing that must be recalculated.

AI for environmental efficiency

AI can help to reduce the impact of farming and heavy industrial operations on the environment. In farming, computer vision systems are emerging that identify weeds in fields of crops to allow weed killer to be sprayed only on them and not the actual crop, consequently generating savings on the amount of weed killer used. This reduces the quantity released into the environment and saves humans from having weed killer-covered produce.

Advanced analytics can make farming much more scientific; for example by analysing weather patterns and soil conditions to identify when to irrigate fields to reduce demand on dwindling water supplies in drought-prone areas.

In some heavy industries, advanced analytics are being used to manage and optimise power consumption. In Chapter 1 I discussed the finding of the EU-funded FUDIPO project, that significant power savings could be achieved through intelligent controls in industrial facilities.

On the subject of power, AI can be used on the supply side of the market too to improve utilisation of green and renewable energy sources. One example is the UK National Grid's investment in AI to understand shifting cloud patterns in order to predict how these might affect solar panels (Shead, 2021). When renewable supplies are uncertain, the National Grid has to keep fossil fuel-based supplies going to make up for any shortfalls. The AI will allow it to get a more accurate view of supplies from renewable sources, and consequently, be able to optimise its supplies and reduce its reliance on fossil fuels.

AI for efficiency of food production and supplies

Another example of AI in farming is analysis of weather patterns and soil conditions to predict the best time to plant seeds, how much fertiliser to use and when, and the optimum time to harvest crops. In terms of the food supply chain, the use of advanced analytics can help organisations plan their supply delivery routes better, to find the optimum routes. This could be used for any part of the delivery network, from planning global shipping routes to local door-to-door deliveries.

Improving health and social care

In healthcare, intelligent health monitoring of patients can be used to predict and prevent problems. In care for the elderly, IVAs can provide help and support to elderly people living alone through voice interactions. When connected to devices through the IoT they can also provide phygital services, such as switching home devices on and off on command or, according to schedules, provide physical security and alerting systems around the home, as well as checking the well-being of the elderly resident. The latter can be done by detecting changes in the patterns of movement around the home. A lack of movement might indicate a fall or other health problems and a relative or carer could be alerted to check on the elderly resident.

AI for business efficiency

AI for business efficiency is a major enabler of the autonomous enterprise. There is much AI that is already embedded in IA solutions, and they are key to building the autonomous enterprise. Accordingly, in the rest of this chapter I focus on IA technologies that provide the means of achieving more efficiency in business operations.

WHAT IS INTELLIGENT AUTOMATION?

IA is a category in the field of technology that covers a range of solutions that help organisations automate business processes that would otherwise be done manually. In their book *Intelligent Automation*, Bornet et al. (2020) provide the following definition:

> IA, also called Hyperautomation, is a concept leveraging a new generation of software-based automation. It combines methods (for example process design, implementation and project delivery, and change management) and technologies (for example machine learning, computer vision, NLP, APIs, RPA) to execute business processes automatically on behalf of knowledge workers. This automation is achieved by mimicking the capabilities that knowledge workers use in performing their work activities (for example language, vision, execution, and thinking and learning).

I covered many of the technologies mentioned in the definition in Chapters 2 and 3 and will expand on them later in this chapter. Other definitions are provided in the Glossary. In this section I focus on automation of business processes.

The processes that are automated using IA often include transactions and data that go across enterprise systems. When not automated, some of these involve people cutting and pasting data from one window on their desktop generated by one business application to another, and in doing so undertaking what is known as swivel chair integration. The bulk of these are transactions involving the handling of structured data, such as names, numbers and prices – the kind of data that can be processed by tools like classic RPA. However, some processes require documents to be checked for references, content in emails and text in chat messages as well as voice calls. These could involve checking a PO, reading a letter of complaint from a customer, details of instructions in a message sent by a banking client and so on. Where language, voice, text and images are involved we are dealing with unstructured data. To automate these types of tasks, intelligent software is needed with language processing capabilities. In fact, intelligent software can handle all kinds of data – structured, semi-structured and unstructured – but they might not be able to connect to some legacy software applications in order to process the data. You might therefore need to connect to those using other technologies such as RPA or through application programming interfaces (APIs).

IA is a software category that is made up of these types of technologies. Some are not inherently intelligent such as a lot of the older crop of RPA software, but many are, including IDP, chatbots and IVAs.

By combining the components of IA you can automate almost any type of transactional process. At the moment the barrier is the level of complexity of the process and the law of diminishing returns. For example, the number of lines of code that you might need to write in order to create a software robot to handle complex tasks can be prohibitive, and the costs of developing and running big-ticket AI solutions could make the business case for such a project less than compelling.

Additionally, IA includes software solutions that use code injection to capture screen information to automate processes through the user interface of applications. These are typically used in contact centres to help automate some of the tasks that agents do.

Also increasingly coming under the umbrella of IA are orchestration software packages that help with the flow of controls between software robots (e.g. RPA) and intelligent solutions as well as machines and people and vice versa. While many RPA vendors have enhanced their built-in workflow and automation controls in their software packages, the third-party variety of orchestration software allows organisations to manage a mixed environment where automations are built on platforms provided by different IA vendors.

IA as a category is expanding and today is often used to refer to process mining and discovery software as well, even though many vendors in this field have been around for a while and quite separately from RPA that led to the creation of IA as a software category. These are included because they allow organisations to take a data-driven and analytical approach to identifying the processes that are good candidates for automation. In other words, they make it possible for organisations to take a data-driven approach to scaling up business process automation.

Figure 5.1 provides a pictorial representation of key components of IA and their most common features. In the following sections, I describe the important components of IA, and provide examples of their use cases, their benefits and their challenges.

THE ROLE OF IA IN BUSINESS EFFICIENCY

In Chapter 1 I shared data from Everest Group's *Enterprise Intelligent Automation Adoption Maturity | Pinnacle Model™ Analysis* report (Everest Group, 2020) where 50 per cent of the Pinnacle Enterprises had achieved cost savings of more than 60 per cent in the process area where the IA technology had been applied. The other 50 per cent reported savings of between 20 per cent and 60 per cent in the same context. Furthermore, out of the remaining group of 41 companies, 29 per cent had also achieved cost savings of over 60 per cent. These are significant figures that are driving automation. I provide more real-life examples of the benefits of IA in the case studies in Chapters 6 to 9. A 2022 version of the same study by Everest Group found that Pinnacle Enterprises were getting better at realising benefits from IA and were doing so faster than before (Everest Group, 2022). The Siemens Global Business Services example in Chapter 6 illustrates the efficiency savings particularly well; the company is saving on time, effort and costs by automating 70 per cent of its service ticket processing; with 7 million tickets generated by its services, the resulting efficiency can be significant.

There are also many non-monetary benefits that can be realised from IA. I cover the key ones in the following sections.

Increased and flexible processing capacity

Automation increases the speed of processing and therefore more work can be done by the organisation, for example more cases processed. Accordingly, capacity to do business is increased. At times of high demand, the automated processes can be operated for longer every day to respond to the demand. Conversely, they can operate at reduced rates when demand is low, providing the enterprise with flexibility and agility.

Figure 5.1 Key components of IA

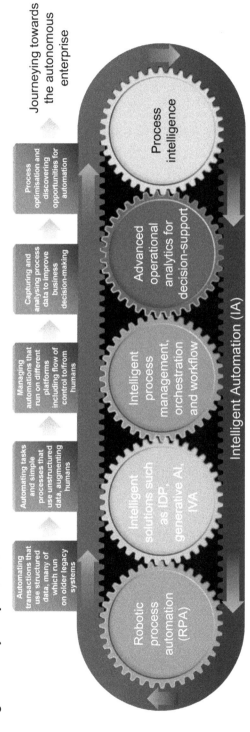

Automating transactions that use structured data, many of which run on older legacy systems

Automating tasks and simple processes that use unstructured data, augmenting humans

Managing automations that run on different platforms including flow of control to/from humans

Capturing and analysing process data to improve business decision-making

Process optimisation and discovering opportunities for automation

Journeying towards the autonomous enterprise

Robotic process automation (RPA)

Intelligent solutions such as IDP, generative AI, IVA

Intelligent process management, orchestration and workflow

Advanced operational analytics for decision-support

Process intelligence

Intelligent Automation (IA)

By combining IA technologies more of each process can be automated and more types of business processes than any individual technology can do on its own.

Common features include:

- Some form of AI e.g. intelligent workflow and controls and/or NLP
- Low code with drag and drop features that make it easy to develop software robots and other types of automations
- Control panels, dashboards and reporting
- Ability to run on premises and on cloud
- Ability to capture process data, providing the basis for analytics, reporting and insights or runtime intelligence

87

Better quality of services

Process-related errors can lead to customer dissatisfaction and even reputational damage. When they occur they are costly to fix because of the duplicated effort required not only to fix the error but also to redo the process and iron out any problems caused by the error, for example claiming a refund back after it was sent to the wrong person. When fully tested, automation can reduce data errors, by copying and pasting data accurately, and consequently minimise the work required to fix any related issues.

Improved adherence to corporate and regulatory requirements and risk reduction

Automations follow the rules that humans give them and, therefore, increase the degree of standardisation of processes. When regulatory and corporate policy requirements are coded in the steps of the automated process, the level of adherence goes up. When data errors are reduced and requirements are coded into the body of the automated processes, risks are mitigated such as the risks of monetary fines and other sanctions due to failure to comply with regulations.

Improved employee engagement

If you automate repetitive processes, you free staff to do the more interesting part of their daily routines such as handling complex cases. There are examples when work that was required to be done out of hours was automated, thus freeing staff from having to do night shifts. You can also augment work to help them do what they do better, with AI-powered technologies, for example next best action guidance and best answers in contact centres. All of these contribute towards more job satisfaction and increased employee engagement.

More data for business intelligence, decision support and innovation

Data provide business insights and you can program automations to capture and log business data for analysis. Reviewing operational data that get captured can show you better or innovative ways of handling customer interactions and improving online services, or increasing personalisation by matching customers to agents, based on their historical data and any affinity shown during past interactions. The same can help with better decision-making as well as increasing transparency about how and why decisions were made with regularly produced business intelligence reports.

Figure 5.2 summarises the benefits of IA.

IA TECHNOLOGIES

In this section I cover some of the main technologies that are used in IA for business process automation. You should think of these as building blocks to create an IA capability for your organisation. I have already mentioned these in the previous chapters of the book. Here, I look at them through an IA lens in a business context.

Figure 5.2 An overview of the benefits of IA

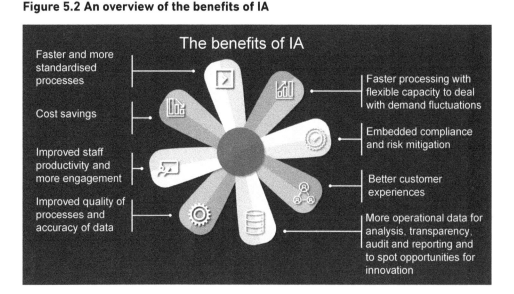

Intelligent document processing (IDP)

Intelligent document processing, sometimes called intelligent content, refers to a group of software solutions that use AI to process enterprise content such as documents, forms, images and emails. IDP turns unstructured data in enterprise content into structured data using a string of capabilities including computer vision – technologies that allow machines to handle visual inputs, text analytics and NLP. The resulting structured data are then fed into other systems for further processing. The steps include image recognition or OCR, indexing and classification of the information, entity recognition and extraction that captures data from the information in the content, and validation against business rules, for example checking the format of a reference in a PO to ascertain its accuracy and compliance with procurement policies and standards. The solutions can then do further processing such as generating reports and insights, and pass the extracted data on to other systems.

Some IDP solutions are complemented with sentiment analysis that assesses the sentiment expressed by the words used in the content, and recommend further action. For example they assess how angry a customer might be based on the words used in a complaint form and then make decisions on its urgency and priority.

IDP is useful to organisations that have to handle large numbers of documents every year, for example insurance companies handling claims that are accompanied by evidence such as photos, or banks doing know your customer (KYC) checks to open accounts for new clients or prior to approving loans and mortgages. The solutions capture key data from the documents submitted by the customer. If these are not in electronic form, they are scanned and digitised. After the information is captured the banks can verify the ID of the customer, checking all the information and comparing it with reference sources, for example address databases. They check the data for discrepancies that could indicate a problem.

IDP solutions for KYC typically finish the process in two ways: if no discrepancy is identified, they complete the process and create a report for a human to review. If an issue is identified they escalate it to a human worker as an exception and then learn from what the human does to resolve the issue and, consequently, enhance their skills.

There are many real-life examples of banks that have significantly reduced their new customer onboarding processes from taking weeks to minutes. The new and highly technology-enabled banks use intelligent solutions to complete KYC processes in minutes compared with some established banks that, using legacy systems, take months. One example is an ex-colleague of mine opening a new business account with one of the new breed of banks, using only his mobile phone while on a taxi ride in London. It did not take him long to have his application approved and account opened. This was in contrast to his business partner's attempt to open an account with a major established UK bank that took many weeks.

The efficiency gain of onboarding clients in minutes compared with months can deliver cost savings, gain more customers and generate additional revenue. It can give the customers better experiences too as shown by the bank account opening example above.

Chatbots and IVAs

The easy accessibility of generative AI solutions like ChatGPT and Google Gemini have significantly boosted interest in intelligent assistants, chatbots and IVAs. They provide a way for people to interact with machines using human languages. They are powered by conversational AI using NLP techniques and its branches of natural language understanding (NLU) and natural language generation (NLG), which allow machines to understand and reply to written or voice-generated human languages (if they also have speech recognition capabilities).

You may well ask what the difference is between chatbots and IVAs. My way of differentiating between them is their levels of intelligence and built-in capabilities.

Some chatbots are simple and rules-based while others are retrieval-based, referencing a database for their answers. The most advanced are those based on LLMs and those can hold longer conversations on multiple subjects depending on their training. Some are hybrids, a combination of rule-based and retrieval-based, using generative AI capabilities to balance the efficiency of predefined responses with the flexibility of generating new content when necessary. Examples of the latter include customer service bots that handle standard queries with a script but use generative AI for more complex questions.

For a description of how different characteristics of LLM-based chatbots can affect the end product please refer to Chapter 3 on generative AI, where I discuss factors such as model parameters, context window, tokens and context window size and what difference they make to the end product.

Many of us have experienced the pain of having to wait on the phone for a contact centre agent to answer our call, while listening to horrible music and repeated recorded messages telling us how valuable our business is to the organisation. Bit by bit AI will help organisations to enhance their services to avoid these kinds of scenarios. They will also empower contact centre agents to be more productive, leading to more efficiency and reduced costs for their operating organisations.

One contact centre operator deployed a text-based chatbot to handle incoming hiring enquiries, mostly of the frequently asked variety. These were taking up a lot of employees' time. By deploying a chatbot to handle the FAQs, the company saw its cost of recruitment reduce by more than 75 per cent per recruit over a six-month period. The same solution has allowed it to more than treble its capacity to handle incoming queries from candidates.

The same company has deployed intelligent tools to automate some of the chat channels that it runs for its clients. Firstly, it identified the opportunities for automation using task mining. It then automated the processes that were identified and recommended by the task mining tool. In its chat channel, in a matter of weeks, it saved in the region of $140,000 by deploying automation using NLP-based classification, and chatbots, resulting in only 4 per cent of staff needing to interact with clients via the channel.

Recent advances in AI and in particular in generative AI are pushing demand for updated contact centre technology. The software market was valued at $42.47 billion in 2023 and is projected to grow to $52.17 billion in 2024 (Fortune Business Insights, 2024). This market is expected to reach $218.31 billion by 2032, with a compound annual growth rate (CAGR) of 19.6 per cent during the forecast period.

The case study in Chapter 7 provides a detailed look at how an English local authority, Calderdale Council, makes use of a chatbot to improve its customer services and how it has helped the council deal with increased demand using a new services model.

Robotic process automation (RPA)

Robotic process automation is a set of software solutions that integrate with other systems through their user interface (UI). This is referred to as non-invasive integration and means no changes to the underlying systems are required to automate a process. Accordingly, RPA mimics the steps that a human user would take to complete a task on a computer. It could be browsing the web to capture information from web pages for price comparisons, or logging in to an enterprise software system with credentials such as username and password to process a transaction.

The word 'robot' refers to the software program that is developed by a programmer using the RPA software. These identify the required controls on the computer screen to mimic human users and work like them, for example to find a text field on the screen and enter data into it. This is where some RPA software use computer vision techniques, to identify the objects on the screen for integration purposes, but many do not. Instead, they use other techniques, such as interacting with user interface elements using selectors or object repositories to identify and manipulate them programmatically.

The use of the term 'robot' gives the impression of some level of machine intelligence, but, as mentioned earlier in this section, this is misleading because these systems have little inherent intelligence. Core RPA solutions come with no machine learning capabilities and are able to process only structured data, the kind of data that you get in a database. They simply go through the instructions that the programmer has embedded in the robot code, step by step.

As time has gone by, RPA software vendors have integrated their solutions with intelligent products, allowing the robots to call routines from those intelligent products to be able to automate more processes. For example, before integration with intelligent solutions, a robot could be programmed to read only the structured data in an email – that is, the sender's name and email address, the subject field and the date and time in the email header. When integrated with an IDP solution, it can also read and make some sense of the unstructured data in the body of the email. Through this type of integration, these software robots are gaining intelligent skills.

Some RPA solutions support APIs to allow the robots to connect to business systems in more ways than the UI. This model has its devotees because the alternative of going through the UI can be a fragile way of connecting to a business system. Changes such as an updated UI layout on an application or an unexpected pop-up window can lead to the robot failing to find the correct data field or object on the screen. The API approach is far more stable, and I have had devoted users of RPA tell me that they connect through APIs where and when possible. That said, I believe the API approach means that the robots are no longer what RPA has to offer. They become more like the traditional system integration technology.

The reason RPA vendors continue to extend the capabilities of their RPA is to be able to offer more functionality and to turn their basic RPA solutions into broad platforms that can automate a wider variety of processes, voice or chat-based, and document-centric as well as transactional processes. Some are working on turning their software robots into agentic AI that can automate specific business processes from end to end.

Styles of RPA

In the world of RPA you will come across some terms that define its style of operation. These include RPA itself, also known as unattended, attended or robotic desktop automation (RDA).

RPA or unattended automation   To some pundits RPA is all about unattended automation. That is when a robot is activated and runs according to predefined schedules or conditions, without a human having to activate it. For example, a robot can be run every night to update a system from multiple spreadsheets. The operation would kick off at a certain time and run on a server in a datacentre based on a predefined schedule.

Another model is to have robots regularly check a queue of tasks to be automated. The status can be indicated by a flag that tells the robot there is work to be done. The robot checks the flag and, if set, checks the source of new information, processes the information by connecting to the required system through its UI and then resets the flag. The source could be a spreadsheet containing new data.

The robot copies the data, then logs in to the relevant business system through its UI, as if a human was signing into the system, and pastes the new data into the appropriate fields. The data could be a packet of information, such as the name and details of a new customer registering an account on an online shop, or a new subscriber to a TV or newspaper service.

Having added the details of a new subscriber to the business system through its UI like a human would, the robot goes back and checks the flag to see if there is more work to be done. The robots can put data in such queues that then activate other robots to take the process further, for example to activate another robot to add the customer details to a CRM system, and in turn activate a third robot to send a text of acknowledgement to the new subscriber. And so, bit by bit we can extend the level of business process automation in the organisation. This is known as unattended RPA, and its devotees believe it is the only true way of automating tasks in order to take the robot out of the human.

Attended RPA   This is when a human activates a robot, from their desktop, to run a certain task. It is also called RDA. Use case examples are prevalent in the contact centre. For example, an agent can activate a robot to update a field in a business application following a call from a customer providing new information or instructions to the company, such as a change of circumstance. The robot could also be activated by a chatbot that has collected the information from a customer either through text in chat messages or through conversational AI, talking to the customer.

The attended RPA robots integrate with other systems in very much the same way as unattended robots – they go through the UI. Some vendors interrogate the target applications and determine what type of connection is best suited to that application.

Some software vendors provide a capability to allow the robot developer to give the attended automation robot an avatar that resides on the user's desktop. The avatar acts as an assistant, and is activated when the tasks that it is programmed to do start. It pops up on-screen and asks if it can complete the task. The avatar can be given a voice interface powered by conversational AI.

I believe, over the next decade, this kind of development will be augmented by generative AI to deliver fully fledged personal IVAs to knowledge workers that are trained in the context of the work and consequently power the next productivity revolution.

Process orchestration

Processes are typically made up of different steps, often needing one step to be fully completed before the next one can be taken. There are also situations that could lead to a process continuing away from its main swim lane in order to satisfy certain conditions, for example, a simple change of address notification by a customer leading to a robot updating the address in several databases. However, if the robot could not easily confirm the identity of the customer, it might need to branch out from the main process flow to double-check the customer's ID and it might need to pass the task to a human to make a decision about the ID, who in turn passes the controls back to the robot. This is what is referred to as human-in-the-loop. The controls then have to be returned to the automated process for the task of address change to be completed. These require workflow, controls and orchestration capabilities.

In the past many companies made use of business process management (BPM) tools that offered features to manage the flow of control between machines and humans. Today we have to manage a more complex mix of robots to humans and to other systems. This is where intelligent BPM solutions and automation-specific orchestration tools have come to the fore. Many RPA solutions already offer workflow and orchestration capabilities within their own systems, but it is the management of controls – across the end-to-end process where RPA and other types of process automation from multiple software vendors might be running – that is needed. This has given rise to a new breed of third-party vendor software tools to help with the running of automated processes in the enterprise. These work across different automation tools and orchestrate the flow of controls and activation of robots.

Process and task mining

Process and task mining capture information from different sources of process data to virtually reconstruct how business is conducted in the enterprise. They then analyse the information to make recommendations for optimising processes, mitigating risks and discovering opportunities for automating more processes. There are two main types of technologies to do this, process mining and task mining, with discovery offered by both. Some vendors offer one or the other and some provide both types of capabilities, either natively in their own platforms or in partnership with other vendors. It is worth asking vendors which or what combination of process and task mining their software solution offers when selecting software, what it takes to prepare for it, to deploy it, how long that is likely to take and what the costs would be.

Process mining
Enterprise software applications underpin many business processes and generate data about those processes in the form of application logs. These logs are great sources of information about how the processes are actually undertaken in the enterprise, for example if they are as standardised as the organisation believes them to be or, if not, what the variations are and what risks to the organisation these represent. I have heard tales of heads of operations almost breaking down when process mining reports have shown them 80 to 100 variations in what they thought to be a highly standardised process. The variations mean unknown risks and costs, and the more of them there are, the higher the risks to the organisation.

In its traditional form, process mining software mines a major business application's logs to discover process steps and branches to virtually reconstruct how processes are undertaken when staff use the application. The process mining software analyses the data to work out where the bottlenecks are and what variations there are in standardised processes. Logs from more than one business application can be mined, but you would have to integrate the captured data for analysis purposes, and that is likely to need significant investment in time and money as a project.

Process mining has been around longer than IA, but it is going through something of a revival on the back of the success of IA. This is because organisations, having automated the most obvious candidate processes, want to know what to automate next. There are manual ways of doing this, but process mining allows organisations to automate the finding of automation opportunities, and so process mining has become an important part of the IA spectrum of technologies.

Task mining

Another approach to getting process-related insights is to capture information from knowledge workers' computers. The approach uses code injection to capture task-related information or computer vision that analyses images of the users' screens. The kind of information that is collected includes what windows they open and what buttons they click. The software then reconstructs the processes based on this information.

The benefits of task mining include identification of bottlenecks or long-winded complex procedures that are not only a source of delays and costs to operations but real pain points for staff, which lead to frustration and job dissatisfaction. These can be identified and addressed. Having virtually reconstructed processes, best candidates for automation can also be identified based on factors such as volumes of transactions, the regularity of patterns of content flowing through the process, and its complexity. Some solutions go further and automatically calculate and report the business case for automating the process based on its characteristics and known costs of implementing automation software.

Unsurprisingly, the concept of task mining can lead to fears of loss of privacy among staff. There are safeguards that can be put in place to address these issues. Measures include:

- ensuring that staff are on board with the project from the start and any data are collected with their permission;

- clear and well communicated objectives for the implementation and transparency on how the data will be used;

- proofs of concepts that show staff what to expect from the technology in practice;

- anonymisation of the data that are captured;

- allowing the staff to see what data are collected about them;

- creating a permitted list of applications that the task mining software can track on the user's desktop to leave other more private applications like personal emails and banking apps out of the equation;

- clearly setting out the data privacy rules that are to be followed by the task mining software.

Once task mining is set up, it captures a huge amount of data. AI is used to analyse the data to join the dots to construct a visual representation of how processes are conducted in the target business area.

The AI in the solution improves deterministic statistical analysis, and supervised algorithms help with pattern matching. As an example of the application of task mining, a contact centre operator implements the technology to find out how long its chat channel agents had to wait for messages to come in. It can also be used to identify what proportion of these chats could be semi-automated based on the pattern and the complexity of the questions that customers posted on the channel.

Some task mining solutions provide a complete view of the interactions between people, the processes and the applications, and the infrastructure that is used to fulfil those processes. They help identify best practice, workload and scheduling issues, and any other points of friction in the process pathway, for example those that might be caused by the IT as well as the workflow. You can think of these types of products as a superset of task mining that extensively support process optimisation and IT modernisation as well as automation.

To conclude this section, here is a summary of what insights process and task mining software can provide by capturing and analysing process information:

- identifying unnecessary steps and bottlenecks in workflows;
- discovering variations in processes and their likely impact on operations and business functions;
- optimising workload assignments and shift patterns;
- identifying candidate processes for automation based on factors such as:
  - frequency and volumes of transactions processed;
  - demand for the process;
  - costs of the operation as is and if the same is automated;
- automatically calculating the business case for automating candidate tasks, having discovered them through the mining;
- uncovering risks, for example where additional steps may be required in processes to improve resilience to system failures or to comply with best practice or regulatory requirements.

Developments in technology lead to new terminologies as well as applications of AI. In the next section I provide an overview of an emerging field increasingly referred to as agentic AI.

AGENTIC AI

Agentic AI, also known as autonomous AI, is a developing field within AI. Agentic AI systems possess a higher level of autonomy within their designated contexts. These systems are capable of learning and adapting from their environments, enabling them to make independent decisions based on their experiences. Designed to handle highly focused complex objectives, agentic AI applies workflows with minimal human intervention. A notable example is the intelligence embedded in autonomous vehicles.

Benefits in enterprise applications

The use of agentic AI in enterprises can significantly extend business process automation and enhance automated operations. For instance, robotic process automation (RPA) can be improved by integrating agentic AI with task mining data analysis. Current applications include recruitment AI agents that sift through CVs, create shortlists, and arrange interviews. Additionally, agentic AI has been utilised to write, test and debug software code. In the near future, commercially available AI agents might be able to devise and implement project plans to achieve specific objectives, such as improving sales or optimising supply chains, by collaborating with other systems or AI agents.

Agentic AI architecture

To achieve their autonomous capabilities, agentic AI systems are built upon a multi-faceted architecture that combines various components and techniques. The mix of learning methods depends on the specialisation of the agentic AI. Firstly, the use of reinforcement learning, along with other methods like supervised and unsupervised learning, allows an agentic AI system to adapt its behaviour continuously. Some systems also learn by observing human behaviour. Secondly, agentic AI may utilise internal world models to make sense of its environment and make decisions on next actions, though not all systems rely on this approach. Thirdly, it has built-in modules that enable it to independently set subgoals and make decisions within its defined context. Some have the ability to prioritise interpretability, allowing them to explain their decisions. This combination empowers agentic AI to learn, plan and make its own choices within a defined context.

Agentic AI, artificial general intelligence (AGI) and ethical development

While agentic AI advances us towards artificial general intelligence (AGI), its capabilities remain limited to specific, predefined objectives. In contrast, human intelligence is open-ended, allowing us to set our own goals and explore new domains independently. Despite these limitations, the responsible development of agentic AI is crucial. Its training should be on comprehensive and representative datasets to ensure its ability to process data without bias. It should be designed, built and run ethically, with human safety and environmental sustainability in mind. Risks of cybercrime and social and economic issues should also be mitigated. These are important aspects to bear in mind to avoid unintended consequences.

Table 5.1 More examples of use cases of IA in different functions and industries

Business function/industry	Use case	How IA can help	Benefits	Challenges
Accounts payable	Many organisations receive invoices by the thousands and in a variety of different formats and layouts. These have to be checked for accuracy and compliance with corporate policies, and referenced against the relevant PO	An IDP solution extracts the required information from invoices, e.g. the quantities, amounts, PO number and cost centre. The data are then automatically checked against reference sources, then passed on either for approval using workflow or for settlement with the IDP directly interacting with the relevant systems or passing the information on to them using RPA. Anything that cannot be confirmed by the IDP solution is flagged as an exception and passed to a human for checking	• faster processing; • increased capacity; • reduced risks of errors; • systematic checking of invoices including checking for fraud; increased business insight as data from operations can be captured quickly, e.g. at the point of invoice settlement rather than waiting for periodic financial reports; • similarly the accounting close process can be made easier with better financial insights; performance data can be captured, e.g. if staff are too slow to deal with workflow-based approval processes	• ensuring the business case stacks up for small to medium-sized operations; fully capturing all the process steps and variations to document for automation and for reference; • optimising processes for automated operations; • ensuring that the automations are maintained and updated when changes happen

(Continued)

Table 5.1 (Continued)

Business function/industry	Use case	How IA can help	Benefits	Challenges
Central government	Ensuring faster benefits claim processing while mitigating risks of fraud	NLP and analytics can be used to check applicants' documents, extracting identity information then checking and verifying the data against reference sources AI can help contact centre staff to deal faster with applications and improve through processing as well as better communications with claimants ID checking and analysis can be augmented with social media information and other sources of data to mitigate risks of fraud, e.g. discover networks of criminal gangs fraudulently claiming benefits using fake identities	• automation speeds up claims application processing; • augmenting staff with AI provides them with information for faster processing of cases; • risks of fraud can be mitigated and costs reduced	• all of the above plus ensuring fair automated processing of claims. This requires testing with a representative dataset and checking of outcomes to feed back into continuous improvements

(Continued)

Table 5.1 (Continued)

Business function/ industry	Use case	How IA can help	Benefits	Challenges
Loan servicing	Loan servicing is a document-intensive process. A lot of text has to be read, and key items of information such as the borrower's name and address, the outstanding amount of loan and interest rates identified, verified and processed	An IDP solution can be used to capture the required information and cross check and validate them against other documents and reference sources	• faster processing of loan servicing cases with automated reading of documents, information capture, referencing and validation; • improved quality of service with reduced data errors; • increased capacity to take on more work and grow revenues;	• as above; • ensuring security of financial information; ensuring that the end solution delivers in accordance with financial regulatory requirements
Healthcare	Settlement of healthcare invoices submitted by different medical workers and for use of hospital facilities to insurance companies can be extremely uncoordinated with delayed and poorly recorded submissions leading to confusion and error	A mix of IDP to read the invoices and capture key data, check for errors and potential fraud, followed by RPA to make the payment, update all the relevant systems and notify all stakeholders: practitioners, hospitals and patients	• data are updated across multiple systems and all parties are kept informed of the current status of payments for the treatment provided; • reduced rates of errors; • mitigating risks of fraudulent claims and increased revenue assurance	• as above

SUMMARY

In this chapter I described how AI can help many industries to run improved operations to achieve efficiency. I provided examples of better informed decision-making, improving the management of the supply chain, and the use of AI to make farming more scientific to save on amounts of weed killer used, water for irrigation and optimal timing of planting, feeding and harvesting crops. I highlighted the use of AI in industrial plants to optimise power consumption. I then focused on business functions and knowledge work and provided an overview of IA for business process automation and the breadth of technologies that fall into this category, mostly powered by AI. I covered agentic AI which is an emerging field in process automation. The technologies that I described provide the quickest way for organisations to adopt AI for business efficiency. There are many off-the-shelf solutions in each of the IA constituent technologies that I have described. I have also provided examples of their use cases.

These pre-packaged technologies fall into the business function toolkits that I described in Chapter 2 and highlighted in Figure 2.1: 'Overview of the types of AI toolkit'. They help organisations to take steps towards becoming autonomous. AI is their major enabler and of advanced digitalisation and process autonomics. We are still at the early stages of this journey, but business pressures mean that we need to learn about the technologies to prepare for the journey.

To wrap up this chapter, Table 5.1 provides a few additional examples of use cases of IA in different functions and industries.

PART 2
CASE STUDIES

In Part 2 I look at a number of case studies of real practical applications of AI in business and healthcare. The case studies show broad uses of AI in daily operations, ranging from customer contact management, to patient care and sales optimisation.

6 THE BIONIC AGENT AT SIEMENS GLOBAL BUSINESS SERVICES

In this case study I describe how Siemens Global Business Services (GBS) uses AI to enhance and augment its customer services. The company has used a variety of technologies to automate its processes, but the case study focuses on what the company refers to as the Bionic Agent. This is an intelligent solution that uses NLP and generative AI to automate the handling of some of the 7 million service tickets that Siemens GBS generates each year, to track, action and manage its clients' enquiries. The solution was developed in-house using Microsoft Azure Services and GPT-4 from OpenAI. It is on course to automate 70 per cent of the work involved in handling the customer enquiries that come into the organisation. Its accuracy is already proven to be over 95 per cent in certain cases, higher than when the work is done manually.

ABOUT SIEMENS GLOBAL BUSINESS SERVICES

Siemens GBS has more than 20 years' experience delivering shared business services to the Siemens group of companies. Today it provides smart and digital services to both internal and external customers. Its current portfolio comprises transactional and expertise-driven services. It employs around 10,000 staff and delivers services to its clients from 11 major delivery locations. These are highlighted in Figure 6.1.

The services that it offers include:

- Finance:
  - Opportunity-to-Cash services including lead generation, sales, order management, cash collection, accounts receivable and after-sales services.
  - Purchase-to-Pay services from purchasing to accounts payable and payment execution and supply chain services.
  - Record-to-Report services from finance records to closing reports.
- HR:
  - Hire-to-Retire services from recruiting to retirement.
  - Temporary personnel including contracting and payroll services.
  - Contingent labour administration and management.
  - Lifelong development and learning.

- Business solutions and services that are expertise-driven and project-based including technical translation services, communications and logistics services.

  - The logistics business includes delivery management.

- Engineering services to provide technology-based solution design and software engineering.

- Project transformation and consultancy services to provide customers with functional process expertise and deliver operational support out of a project management pool.

Figure 6.1 The global service network of Siemens GBS (Source: Siemens GBS)

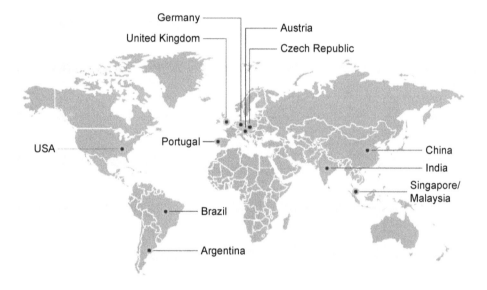

THE BUSINESS CONTEXT

As an organisation that started as a shared services centre, efficiency has always been important for Siemens GBS. The means of achieving it have traditionally included labour arbitrage, centralisation of services, specialisation and scale, which lead to savings through synergies, sharing of resources and standardisation. Today, there is increased focus on technology as an enabler of efficiency and innovation to drive business outcomes faster while maintaining the benefits of the shared services model. To this end, Siemens GBS is increasingly taking advantage of technology. Each year, it runs programmes for service modernisation to improve capacity and straight through processing. The company sees this as a necessity to stay ahead in a world where disruption can happen very quickly. New players can emerge with novel business models powered by technology that quickly capture a share of the market, leaving established corporations in a tailspin as they struggle to modernise legacy systems and service models that are difficult to change.

One of the fields of technology that Siemens GBS has invested in is IA to improve process and service efficiency. In 2019 and 2022, it took part in *Enterprise Intelligent Automation Adoption Maturity | Pinnacle Model Analysis*, a study by Everest Group (2020, 2022) to identify large companies that had developed best-in-class IA capabilities and were achieving the best outcomes. Siemens GBS did consistently well in the two studies with Everest Group positioning them as a leader in both.

Siemens GBS started implementing AI technologies in 2017 and by 2019 it had automated over 450 processes. Examples included an intelligent Inventory Recommender that used machine learning and predictive analytics combined with RPA to optimise stock levels and subsequently reduce the total inventory value for its clients by more than 30 per cent. It also provided automation of logistics for parts. Other examples include its use of IoT combined with data analytics and RPA to enable predictive machine maintenance, automated invoice processing and IT incident management where RPA robots capture incident information from different systems and create tickets in the service management software.

THE BIONIC AGENT FOR SERVICE TICKET PROCESSING

The scale of Siemens GBS's operations around the globe has resulted in the company having to deal with millions of service tickets generated each year. The service tickets are created following every customer enquiry, be it by phone, email or via other interaction channels. These add up to more than 7 million tickets each year. The enquiries come in mostly by email despite Siemens GBS having implemented self-service portals where its clients can access service information and see the status of work in progress. Additionally, it has deployed chatbots provided on the self-service portals to answer customer enquiries. The figure of 7 million tickets a year excludes the customer interactions that have been completed by the chatbots.

Another channel operated by Siemens GBS is email provided with function-specific mailboxes, for example for specific finance or HR services. The majority of all enquiries come in through this channel. Contact by phone is also supported. To keep track of interactions and their status and management, every customer contact that is made via the phone is logged in the ticketing system manually by staff.

The Bionic Agent is cloud-based and was developed to automate the process of handling these enquiries, to make the customer services faster and more efficient. In 2023, it was enhanced with generative AI with a direct interface to a private instance of GPT LLM. More on the technology of the Bionic Agent follows in the next section.

The emails describing the nature of the enquiries have to be read, the context understood and appropriate action taken or planned. These can be simple questions, for example a client asking what the status of a PO is, or they can be more complex, such as an email informing the organisation that a whole chain of approvals is to be updated as a result of personnel changes. Sometimes they come in with documents attached, the content of which can include text and image, all of which have to be looked at, understood and taken into account when handling the enquiry.

Under the hood of the Bionic Agent

The Bionic Agent uses NLP and generative AI to handle the incoming unstructured data, that is the text in the emails, tickets or documents. It does what a human would do: it reads and classifies the information in the text. By leveraging LLMs and vision language models (VLMs), today the Bionic Agent also handles contents of attachments including text and images, like a screenshot of an application. It then interprets the data in the context of the ticket and any attachment to action the next step, for example activate the relevant workflow or an RPA agent. It was developed in stages in-house, initially in the Purchase-to-Pay (P2P) function to simply identify the exact nature of the incoming request and to send it to the right group of staff for processing. Siemens GBS has extended the software functionality over time to do more, including to Record-to-Report (R2R), Opportunity-to-Cash (O2C) and Hire-to-Retire (H2R). The Bionic Agent can work in different capacities, for example as a first line support agent or providing basic frequently asked questions services. Beyond the first line of support, queries get routed to humans. Last fiscal year, the Bionic Agent processed around 1 million tickets working 24×7, always keeping an eye on the inbox for new emails and tickets.

Thanks to its generative AI capabilities, the Bionic Agent also provides a set of microservices including entity extraction from the prompt within guidelines (identifying key information from the text), document summarisation and translation, generative AI assistance that through reasoning can decide how best to help the client. Furthermore, the zero-shot prompt enables the Bionic Agent to answer customer questions through its general knowledge and reasoning without having been trained in the subject of the answer.

To illustrate its capabilities, imagine a client asking for a copy of an invoice. By 'digesting' the text of the client's enquiry, the Bionic Agent works out who the client is, which invoice it needs to retrieve, what the amount in question is and so on. It then gets all that information from the ticketing platform that it is integrated with. Next, it generates the email reply to the customer and attaches a copy of the invoice. The final click of the send button is done by a human who checks the reply for accuracy. This step can be automated too but is there for quality checks.

The key capabilities of the Bionic Agent include the use of a number of algorithms as follows.

Classification
Powered by text mining, the first algorithm indexes and classifies the enquiry based on its content. Through extensive training of the model with historical data, Siemens GBS reports that it has achieved over 90 per cent accuracy in the classification capability. According to the company, the algorithm has made the decision-making more objective than when humans do it. This is because of the machine's ability to rapidly relate the information to a huge volume of historical data, to compare the context and classify the incoming customer enquiry. The Siemens GBS team believes this aspect clearly demonstrates how AI can augment human activity. Some of their human service centre

agents have learnt from the decisions that the machine has made, and consequently become more objective in their decision-making.

Prioritisation

After the classification, another algorithm prioritises the tickets. This is based on the nature of the enquiry and the estimated urgency. To do this, sentiment analysis is also undertaken to work out the urgency as perceived by the client based on the language used in the email or other interactions. Each ticket is then prioritised and gets assigned a response time within service level agreements (SLAs).

Entity extraction

The third machine learning model is used to extract data (entities) and decide what action is to be taken in response; for example in a procurement context, identifying the PO number, or if the approvals need changing, extracting who was the original approver and who is the new one. Other activities include data validation using predefined taxonomies (categories) and rules.

After the entity extraction the appropriate workflow is activated, and all the relevant information is passed to the automated solution that services that workflow. This can be an RPA robot that takes the information and updates the field in the relevant business system, for example changing the name of the approver in the purchasing system. Or it can be a direct data update to a business system using RESTful application programming interfaces (REST APIs).

In this way, using NLP, unstructured information is converted to structured data that can be automatically put into the relevant business system. That data update might complete the activity that was needed in response to the ticket being generated or it might activate another chain of processes, many of which are automated too, for example an update sent to a supplier.

Completion

The final step is to go back to the client who raised the service request with a response. This too is partially automated with the information being provided to a human agent to be checked. The generative AI enables the Bionic Agent to produce the text of the response to go out to the client, following approval by a human. Siemens GBS made the decision to have humans oversee this final customer interaction. It refers to it as its quality gate where humans-in-the-loop check the work that has been done by the machine.

The solution development

Siemens GBS has a large technology group as well as an innovation team that comes up with ideas for new solutions to enhance the company's services. The group can also respond to demand from the business to deal with their specific requirements. In this case, the service ticket handling was a very high-volume process that took a lot of manual effort. Consequently, the team assigned to the project scanned the market for out-of-the-box technologies that were available at the time, but they needed to develop a capability that offered them reusability. They also wanted a cloud-based and highly scalable solution. As a result, they selected Microsoft's Azure platform and in 2023 added a connection to GPT-3.5 LLM supplied by OpenAI. This has since been upgraded to GPT-4. The architecture has three layers: the Azure platform, a generative AI layer that handles classification and extraction, and an orchestration layer that is used to coordinate the running of automations. The project team worked with Microsoft on the development of the solution.

In addition, the team leveraged AI expertise and experience within the corporate technology group as well as their teams in Portugal and Czechia.

Having set up the project and created the development team, it took nine months to build the minimum viable product. Initially, it just classified the information captured from the service tickets and routed them to the right teams for action. They ran a proof of concept for six weeks and saw that they could unlock higher-value work by speeding up ticket processing times and freeing up staff from having to do that initial task. They then added the entity extraction and then the rest. They had to ensure that the Bionic Agent was secure and that it complied with corporate digital and HR policies, International Organization for Standardization (ISO) information security standards, and regulations such as the General Data Protection Regulation (GDPR). There was a lot of learning through trial and error to get the right algorithm and to increase its accuracy.

The core engine is NLP, and the design is such that it allows the Bionic Agent to be applied to other requirements. Since it has been augmented with generative AI capabilities, it automates much of the process of handling service tickets, including all the steps of classification, prioritisation, entity extraction, task completion and response preparation. In future, it might be trained to extract other data and be applied to other use cases in the company.

The benefits

Siemens GBS has generated significant benefits from the Bionic Agent already. Where it is deployed, service ticket resolution effort has been 70 per cent automated with roll-out to more areas of business planned. The accuracy of ticket classification and entity extraction is over 95 per cent in some cases. It is automating more than 10,000 hours of work every year, completing tasks end to end. The solution today handles tickets for more business teams inside and outside GBS.

Moreover, with the addition of generative AI, the Bionic Agent can develop new business capabilities quickly through prompt engineering. This speeds up development by several weeks. Therefore new features can be added to the solution in three to four weeks. For example, the task of providing a copy of an invoice, mentioned earlier, can become a standard task offered by the product: an extension to its catalogue of services made easily possible through prompt engineering. This is done by a developer prompting the Bionic Agent to do the same task over and over again until it learns all there is about the task and it becomes one of its standard services.

The Bionic Agent has enabled its staff to work on higher-value processes such as complex cases that cannot be automated or analysis of customer contact data to improve services. Additionally, the company has built the foundations for an intelligent solution that can be adapted and reused to speed up and enhance other services. This work is ongoing, and we expect to see more efficiencies generated by Siemens GBS in the near future.

The company has also increased its AI skills and will be able to develop new products in its pursuit of new technology solutions to innovate and stay ahead of the competition.

SUMMARY

In this chapter we learnt how Siemens GBS developed its Bionic Agent to speed up the processing of service tickets that are generated in response to customer queries. The solution is based on NLP and generative AI. It automates 70 per cent of the ticket-handling processes. The rest is completed by staff who check the work that has been done before completing the task associated with each ticket.

The Bionic Agent was developed in-house based on Microsoft Azure and GPT-4 by OpenAI, deployed on cloud for scalability.

This case study demonstrates two major themes: firstly that organisations can turn large parts of their business processes into autonomous operations while still having people involved, not only to develop the solutions, but also to manage and monitor the automated processes, to handle more complex tasks, as well as to deal with direct customer interactions. Secondly, that as new technology comes along, it too can be applied and built into the fabric of modernised services. In this case it is the addition of generative AI to an already intelligent, NLP-powered solution. This is a good example of enterprises' journeys towards the autonomous enterprise, with many destinations along the way when additional capabilities are added as they become possible.

Moreover, this is exactly how I believe most knowledge work in the enterprise will be delivered in the future. The change will happen as part of the evolution of services rather than a revolution because it will happen by degrees as intelligent technologies are enhanced and improved.

There are several other important lessons to learn from Siemens GBS's Bionic Agent:

- It can augment the work of the human agents, for example help them to become more objective in process-related decision-making.
- Different types of AI can be combined and used, and those, in turn, can tap other technologies to scale up process automation. Consequently, the benefits that can be derived from it are boosted, for example AI with RPA leading to 70 per cent of service ticket processing being automated.
- AI-based solutions can be developed with reusability in mind. They can be repurposed to operate in different business contexts, for instance, even in one function area that can handle POs as well as invoice enquiries.
- If you cannot find the solution that you need in a business function toolkit described in Chapter 2, you can develop your own with much of the infrastructure needed provided by AI platform vendors.

Finally, Siemens GBS is not intimidated by the complexity of smart technology. Its approach is all about trialling things with a proof of concept, building a skills base, learning by doing and building on successes. This is an approach that I cannot recommend enough.

7   RETAINING THE HUMAN TOUCH AT CALDERDALE COUNCIL

In this case study I look at the use of an IVA at Calderdale Council in England. In my view the way that this project was undertaken exemplifies application of best practice. It shows how a joined-up, inclusive approach supported by executives and with good stakeholder communication can deliver great success. Another important aspect of this case study is that it shows how intelligent solutions can be enhanced post-deployment to respond to changing conditions and requirements. Finally, it demonstrates that to some degree the solutions can be simple and updated by non-technical staff.

BACKGROUND

Local government organisations around the world are under constant pressure to provide services to satisfy increasing demand while their budgets are cut. Calderdale Council is no exception, and consequently, it has had to undertake major programmes of work to reduce the cost of services while at the same time improving the customer experience. The style of interactions with citizens has also been changing, with demand for digital channels going up.

In 2018, the council started to implement an IVA. It had already refreshed its website and introduced web forms. It had also operated a live chat channel that was first introduced in 2014. The IVA was to advance its digitalisation and omnichannel support objectives. Given that the council serves customers with varied needs, it was essential for it to continue to provide an option for citizens to interact with human advisors for open and empathetic conversations. Ensuring that the option to chat with a person is always available is one reason the automated channel has been successful. Customers have been free to choose rather than feeling constrained by the automation.

In 2014, 70 per cent of customer contacts were over the phone. By March 2020 that figure had fallen to 30 per cent. Today, most of the council's services can be accessed through digital and self-service channels. Over the same period customer satisfaction also improved. Careful implementation, led from the top, with a keen eye on the business benefits and the human angle have produced these impressive results.

ABOUT CALDERDALE COUNCIL

Calderdale Council serves approximately 210,000 citizens in Yorkshire, England. It is a metropolitan borough council so it provides a wide range of local services from libraries

Figure 7.1 Geographic area covered by Calderdale Council (Source: Calderdale Council)

and leisure centres to road maintenance and waste services. It employs 2,600 people and has been on a mission to transform the major towns in the borough. Figure 7.1 shows the geographic area covered by the council.

THE BUSINESS CONTEXT

Local government organisations in England have been under intense budgetary pressure. From 2011 to 2018 central government funding to all local authorities was reduced by 49 per cent (National Audit Office, 2019) in real terms against a backdrop of increasing demand for services due to an ageing population. The trend has continued since. In 2024 the National Audit Office (NAO, 2024) reported that while the 2024–25 local government finance settlement provided a £4.5 billion increase in funding for local authorities compared to 2023–24, it has not reduced financial pressures felt by local government due in part to rising costs and increased demand across a range of services.

Other organisations can adopt radical policies to reduce the level of service to meet cost constraints, but social and legislative pressures mean that is not an option for local government. The only option is to carefully balance reducing costs with the need to ensure that statutory duties and the needs of society are still met. In technology terms, this means increasing automation of business processes for efficiency while ensuring that there is no barrier to the empathetic human contact that many citizens need when they contact their local authority.

The council responded with a programme of improvement covering all aspects of customer access. Digital by choice became its benchmark for service provision with chat a major channel for online engagement and improving the customer experience. These requirements drove the introduction of the virtual assistant for handling short transactional interactions, while keeping access to contact centre agents open.

INTRODUCING VIRA

Having successfully deployed live chat in 2014, the council decided to take the next step to introduce an IVA to support self-service and provide consistently high-quality experiences to customers no matter when they contacted the council (e.g. outside normal working hours). The IVA was to help website visitors by signposting them to online forms and the My Account customer portal.

A project team was set up in November 2018 staffed with the contact centre team leader and advisors, plus staff from the council's IT and web teams. They also engaged an external partner to provide development and related professional services. The IVA that Calderdale Council developed is called VIRA (Virtual, Interactive, Responsive Assistant) and it has been trained and implemented to respond to questions in certain categories. It continues to operate today signposting and handling simple queries of website visitors.

There are a few points to mention about VIRA. First of all, the customer has the option to chat with an advisor at any time. The council considers it very important that their customers use the virtual assistant because it is convenient but that they never feel stuck in an automated channel. Secondly, the whole customer access strategy fits together, meaning that web chat was implemented to help keep customers on a self-service channel. This also means that the council can get insights to understand when customers break off from that channel and choose to use the phone or visit the council in person. These jump-off points can be traced and fixed.

Alongside website improvements there was a significant effort put into improving the large number of web forms needed on the site and ensuring that the high-volume forms were part of an end-to-end process both within the council and from the customer's perspective. The council continues to invest in more forms and smarter ones today.

The implementation

The first implementation was a pilot to help with council tax enquiries that came in via its human-operated chat channel. The business area was chosen because it had the most demand across all channels per year. Popular customer queries and outcomes provided by the agents were identified and categorised for training purposes, to guide customers to fill in an online form, refer them back to the office and email a response or complete the enquiry during the chat. Additionally, the project team had to pre-emptively think of all the likely questions that customers might ask VIRA and the variations in the words that they might use.

The first version of VIRA was released to a community of users. These were still internal to the council and its associated agencies and not the public. VIRA went through six to seven weeks of testing in the community. The testing demonstrated that it could handle the type of vocabulary that was used by real people in real circumstances. A lot of the set-up of VIRA and its training had been informed by previous chat histories, that is, words and sentence constructs that people had used prior to VIRA when the chat channel was operated by the contact centre personnel.

While the initial parts of the configuration set-up and training were undertaken by the council's service partner working in collaboration with the most experienced contact centre agents, post-implementation, staff were trained to add new words and intents to its vocabulary.

VIRA is also available on smartphones and tablets as well as Calderdale Council's website. While vocabulary updates can be made by editing text, each change requires testing before taking the enhanced VIRA into production.

When the COVID-19 pandemic hit the country back in 2020, the contact centre advisors had to respond very quickly to changes in both policies and structures. This ability to update VIRA's capabilities fast to handle new types of enquiries from citizens was a great advantage.

During the implementation, the council developed a short customer survey to be offered on every chat to gauge customer reaction and satisfaction with the channel. During the pilot, the team sent out a new weekly newsletter to all customer services advisors and other stakeholders to keep them abreast of VIRA's development and implementation and the potential benefits that it would bring to their part of the service.

VIRA typically connects the customer to a web resource, to information or a web form for example. The majority of questions are answered satisfactorily in this way. The council has built safeguards into the process: certain topics, such as bereavement or disability, automatically connect the customer to a human advisor.

Scaling up VIRA

The development that started in 2018 went live in March 2019. With the foundations in place, and having gone into production for council tax chat services, further work could then proceed on enhancing VIRA to take in more service areas. Council tax was soon joined by waste services. At this point the world changed as COVID-19 hit in early 2020 and that meant the council having to make reactive changes to policies and procedures quickly, often with a need to implement the changes overnight. As mentioned previously, VIRA could be rapidly updated by staff in the customer contact operation with no need to refer to technical departments for these updates; they could be approved, tested and released in a matter of hours. By this stage in the development of VIRA, around 70 per cent of customer queries were resolved directly, with about 30 per cent of the sessions being referred to an advisor.

To progress further, the implementation team felt that some of the interactions could benefit by being made more conversational. Subsequently, after some discussion and assessments of requirements, it was decided to change the underlying product to a more powerful digital assistant. Furthermore, the team increased their focus in several areas:

- Determining the best path for an individual customer to take by using the information in their questions and consequently directing them to the answers in the right context. For example the question 'What is my balance?' can be interpreted in several different ways. The context has to be taken into account before the customer starts the dialogue to determine their council tax balance when they might have meant the balance on their rent account.

- A more conversational path to be taken when needed to resolve ambiguity by asking the customer further questions and then directing them to the right resources.

- With social media becoming ever more popular, the council was keen to provide support for a wide variety of channels starting with their own website, Facebook Messenger and text (SMS).

The upshot was a renewed version of VIRA with the ability to answer more questions in the target subject areas.

Initially, frequent team meetings were held to review VIRA's interactions and responses to enhance its performance. Later the meetings were held on an ad hoc basis when additional support was needed, typically to do with language and recognition of intents.

A set of dashboards were implemented to allow the team to monitor intents. These showed how answers matched to intents and those escalated to an agent, and which were the most popular expressions. The latter dashboard highlighted expressions that VIRA had issues with and provided further drill down analysis to help with enhancing its performance.

Under the hood of the solution

VIRA uses NLP to interpret what the customer is saying. Initially it was based on a simpler virtual assistant technology from a large software vendor. Later, it was moved to a more powerful digital assistant provided by the same vendor. The upgrade allowed more flexibility in the way conversations were handled. Figures 7.2 and 7.3 show the solution overview and a high-level view of typical customer journeys.

Figure 7.2 The solution overview

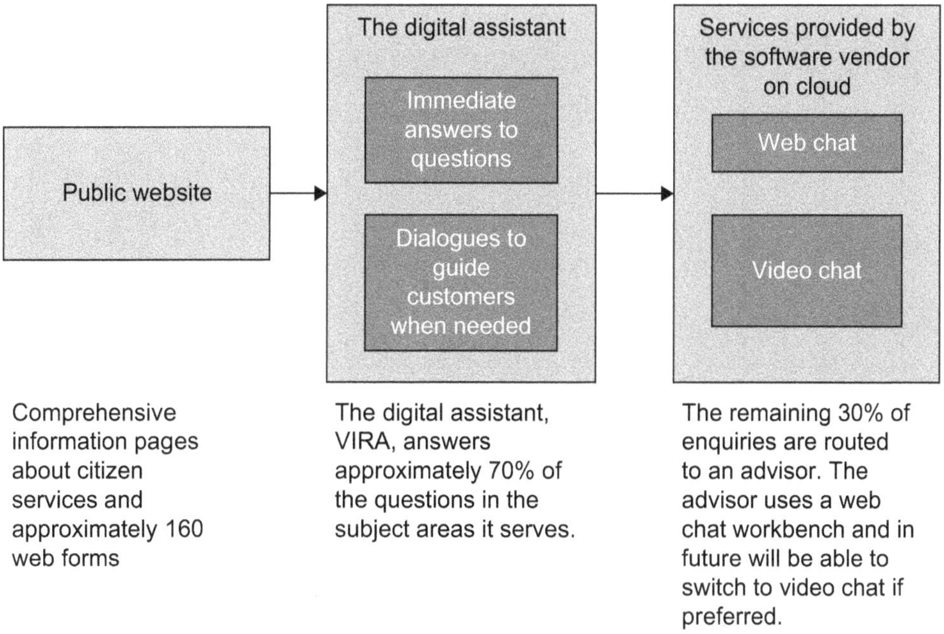

Public website	The digital assistant — Immediate answers to questions; Dialogues to guide customers when needed	Services provided by the software vendor on cloud — Web chat; Video chat
Comprehensive information pages about citizen services and approximately 160 web forms	The digital assistant, VIRA, answers approximately 70% of the questions in the subject areas it serves.	The remaining 30% of enquiries are routed to an advisor. The advisor uses a web chat workbench and in future will be able to switch to video chat if preferred.

The solution development

I particularly like the approach that Calderdale Council took to develop the solution. It is a great example of best practice that led to the council's success. Firstly, a strong internal team was mobilised with good executive support. Secondly, responsibility was devolved to the team of people that had to operate the end solution, that is, the contact centre team. This was very important given that they were the team that after the implementation would have to carry out changes to the NLP in VIRA to ensure that it could deal well with words, terms and language usage as a whole.

Figure 7.3 Customer journeys guided by VIRA

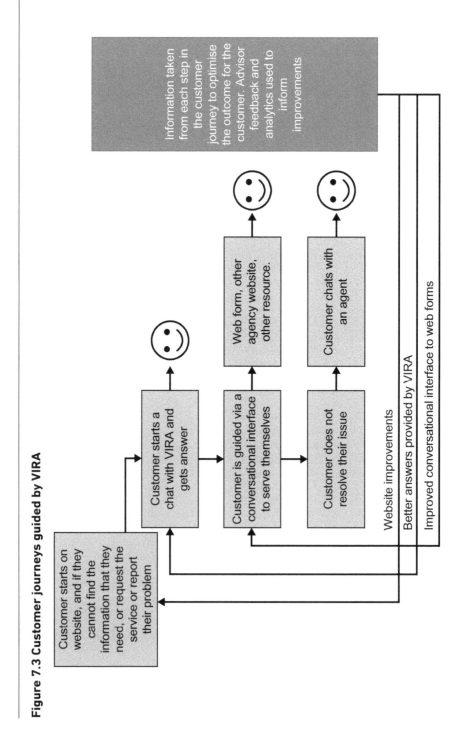

Thirdly, the council also ensured that all stakeholders were kept informed of developments and progress. They instigated a customer survey to understand how customers were finding the service and their satisfaction levels.

Fourthly, there was a complete feedback loop that was used to gather performance and satisfaction data to feed back into enhancements to VIRA and the service as a whole. Furthermore, VIRA was very much a part of the bigger picture of digitalisation of council services to make it possible to provide excellent self-service experiences for citizens.

There was a good partnership with the council's service providers and suppliers as well. The dynamics worked well powered by good communication – another important part of best practice.

Each phase of the project was measured against success criteria. Many of these related to efficiency, but customer satisfaction was measured at each stage, and the internal stakeholders were also carefully managed.

The benefits

The key benefit of the overall programme was that telephone contact was reduced from 70 per cent of all customer contact to 30 per cent, with improved customer satisfaction. The benefits are clear, with the average cost of a phone call across all local authorities having been between £3 and £4 at the time. Further benefits were then achieved by 'catching' complex situations before they became difficult both in well-being and financial terms for the customer and the council. These benefits had to be balanced at all times with maintaining customer satisfaction in the service. Unsurprisingly, many customers want to get on to a council website, get the information that they need or make the request or report they want and then get on with their daily lives.

Today, VIRA continues to help the council maintain a high level of call resolution during the first point of contact. That is, 85 per cent of customer enquiries continue to be fully handled during their first contact with the council today. Figure 7.4 summarises some of the feedback about the service.

VIRA today

Since the pandemic, the council's objective of transforming the majority of its services into digital has been largely achieved. Furthermore, the council's offices have re-opened for in-person enquiries. Nonetheless, VIRA continues to signpost visitors and handle simple enquiries on the website. It also provides extensive support for specific campaigns when the council knows that it is going to receive a lot of enquiries. One such example was the council's introduction of a tip permit system for its residents that led to a higher volume of contact in customer services than usual. In addition to its daily operations, VIRA was used to successfully support the service team as queries for tip permits started to flood in.

VIRA's technology is very powerful and it could do a lot more. Today, the council is successfully developing its internal capabilities and supplier partnerships to start to tap VIRA's additional capabilities. Plans include access to human service experts through a

Figure 7.4 Examples of customer feedback about the service

"I was reluctant to proceed when I knew I wasn't speaking to a human but I have been pleasantly surprised"

"Thank you for the advice, I will use this service again"

FEEDBACK

"Great service, thank you"

"Great that I have been able to have my question answered even when your offices are closed"

video chat channel set up in the council's satellite offices. VIRA's underlying technology is powerful and can support such operations.

SUMMARY

In this chapter we learnt how Calderdale Council applied best practice to judiciously deploy AI in the form of a virtual assistant. The benefits are very clear, but, importantly, the deployment was done as part of an overall joined-up programme that included many website improvements and better online forms. The result was that contact centre personnel were able to better address changing and urgent requirements heightened by the pandemic.

The development took place in incremental steps, each of which was measured against success criteria. Although one of the prime objectives was efficiency, other criteria included customer and employee satisfaction. Informed by feedback from customers and the analytics, incremental improvements were implemented to get better answers and cover more complex queries.

The council intends to maintain the continuous improvement cycle and to extract more benefits from VIRA. It is building on its capabilities to handle new developments and it expects to tap VIRA's advanced features further in future.

8 IMPROVING STROKE CARE USING AI AT THE ROYAL BERKSHIRE NHS FOUNDATION TRUST

You don't have to be an AI scientist to enjoy reading about new AI developments that are good for humankind and the planet. An excellent example is the use of AI at the Royal Berkshire NHS Foundation Trust (RBFT) in Reading, England, to examine CT scan images of brains of stroke patients. The software is able to identify the extent of damage and to highlight early changes that might not be visible to the physician. It is not a diagnostic tool but helps doctors to decide the best care pathways for stroke patients, as well as speeding up their treatment. It addresses one of the main obstacles to faster treatment of stroke patients, and that is the possible lack of neuroradiology imaging expertise on site when patients present out of hours. By augmenting the general physicians' decisions and accelerating treatment along the appropriate stroke pathway, the risks of patients suffering permanent brain damage or death are minimised.

It has been used at RBFT since March 2020 and it has already helped to improve care as part of a series of measures that include increased collaborative working with a network of hospitals in the Thames Valley in England. The AI software has boosted the ability of the network to share scan images on hand-held devices and smartphones to allow emergency non-specialist doctors to connect with specialists out of hours. The combination of these factors means that care compared with before the deployment has improved. Initial assessments of results showed:

- Door-in-door-out time, the time that it takes to get a patient diagnosed and sent to a specialist hospital, almost halved from 140 minutes to 79 minutes.
- Referral time shrank by 75 per cent from 77 minutes to 44.
- Most importantly, patient outcomes have seen a significant improvement, with initial data indicating a tripling of the rate of those who achieve independence after a major stroke.

ABOUT RBFT

The RBFT is one of the largest NHS trusts in England. It has multiple sites across Berkshire, the largest of which is Royal Berkshire Hospital in Reading. It provides specialist services such as cancer, dialysis and eye surgery to a wider population across Berkshire and beyond its borders. Where stroke care is concerned it has joined forces with other trusts to create a regional stroke collaboration partnership that is known as the Thrombectomy Innovation and Transformation Network (TITAN). The other hospitals in the partnership are located in Aylesbury, High Wycombe, Milton Keynes, Northampton, Oxford and Swindon.

RBFT has a 'digital by default' vision to extend its use of digital technologies to improve health outcomes.

THE HEALTHCARE CONTEXT

Stroke is a devastating condition that, according to the Stroke Association (n.d.), strikes every five minutes in the UK, affecting 100,000 people each year. It can happen anywhere, often in the patient's local community where specialist stroke care might be out of reach. Time is of the essence to save a person from disabling long-term effects or even death.

Treatment involves intravenous thrombolysis (IVT) but in the case of large vessel strokes, patients are likely to need mechanical thrombectomy (MT) as well to remove any resulting blood clots. This is a specialist treatment that only some hospitals are able to perform.

Availability of specialists such as radiologists with the right skills at the time of treatment can also make a big difference to the outcome. Accordingly, there are two care pathways for stroke patients highlighted in Figure 8.1 (Nagaratnam, 2020).

In Figure 8.1, in the mothership model, the patient is taken direct to the specialist hospital where full stroke treatment can be offered including both IVT and MT, following a computerised tomography angiography (CT/CTA) scan. In the other pathway, the drip and ship model, the patient is taken to the nearest hospital and a CT scan of their head is taken to assess the type of stroke and to administer IVT. Patients diagnosed with large blood clots who will need MT have to be transferred to a specialist unit as quickly as possible. Roughly 2 million neurons die in the brain every minute as a result of large blood clots starving them of oxygen.

Diagnosis of a large vessel occlusion (LVO) using CTA images requires skills and experience. During normal working hours, radiologists and stroke specialists can work collaboratively to assess the extent of the damage caused by the stroke shown in the CT or CTA scans. The need for accurate and speedy diagnosis remains and is particularly acute when an emergency happens out of hours. This is when the emergency department doctor or non-specialist doctor needs to be able to reach the right specialists to consult them, and that may take some time. There is also the speed of transferring medical images electronically to the specialists' laptops, if they are working remotely because of their shift patterns. In some cases this can take 20 minutes or more but in the case of stroke treatment, every minute matters. The speedier the treatment the more likely a patient will recover and return to normal life.

The e-Stroke Suite

As part of its stroke care enhancements, RBFT had already joined others in the TITAN partnership to streamline the drip and ship model. As well as optimising some of the

Figure 8.1 The stroke thrombectomy pathway (Source: Nagaratnam, 2020)

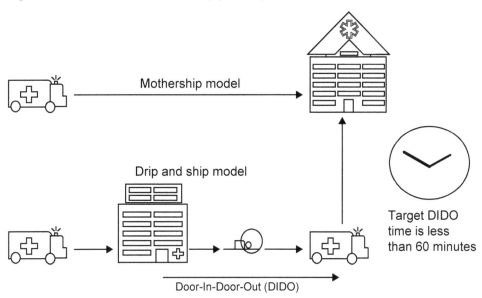

manual steps taken in patient care along this pathway, in 2019–20 it started to examine the possibility of using AI to help doctors diagnose CT and CTA scans. The aim of adding AI to the care pathway was to speed up diagnosis for those needing essential MT.

In March 2020, RBFT started to trial the use of AI. They implemented e-Stroke Suite developed by Oxford-based Brainomix Ltd. This is a set of intelligent tools for non-contrast CT and CTA brain scans. It is a decision-support tool that helps doctors to assess the damage caused by stroke. Since its deployment, it has been used in scans of thousands of patients at RBFT, and physicians believe that it provides very high accuracy for proximal vessel occlusion in the anterior circulation type of LVO – that is, blood clots in front of the brain. It is not designed to detect other abnormalities such as tumours – it has to be used in the right context.

Close collaboration with all stakeholders from the outset was essential. These included the stroke specialists and the emergency department, the radiologists, the hospital IT departments, the teams in charge of treatment and information governance, and the supplier.

In 2020, the implementation of the cloud version of e-Stroke was fast tracked because of the COVID-19 pandemic, which resulted in stretched hospital resources and unavailability of specialists due to self-isolation. This allowed images to be made available on smartphones at high speed so that specialists could see them no matter where they were, travelling to and from the hospital or isolating at home after coming into contact with COVID-19.

While RBFT pioneered the use of the e-Stroke system in Reading, and rolled it out in March 2020, five other partner hospitals in the Thames Valley followed suit in June 2020. These were:

- Milton Keynes University Hospital;
- Wycombe General Hospital;
- Great Western Hospital;
- Northampton General Hospital;
- John Radcliffe Hospital (JRH), Oxford.

JRH in Oxford is one of the neuroscience specialist centres that provides thrombectomy services to the other hospitals in the Thames Valley area. The implementation of e-Stroke servers at all these hospitals allows them to share CT scanned images quickly for patients that are being referred. The sharing of images is done within data privacy regulations.

UNDER THE HOOD OF THE TECHNOLOGY

The Brainomix technology is based on neural networks and deep learning. It is trained like a doctor to analyse images to spot signs of cerebral bleeding and serious or irreversible damage. The company uses images and data from around the world to train its algorithms.

It can identify ischaemic changes to the brain (caused by the lack of blood and oxygen) as well as LVO and collateral vessel density in the anterior circulation, front of the brain. It uses a heatmap to show the regions of the brain that have been affected, and within each region to the pixel, whether it has detected any damage. In other words, e-Stroke assesses the patient for cerebral bleeding. It then shows the doctor any irreversible brain damage and LVO. It measures and highlights the damage and at-risk tissue.

e-Stroke can also handle multiphase CTA to detect the core – that is, where the most damage is caused by the stroke – and the effect on collateral blood flow around the core. It creates a composite image from the different phases of the multiphase CTA to show the blood flow, highlighting where the blockages are, as shown in Figure 8.2. Consequently, it can provide temporal information to reveal slower collateral blood flow.

The benefits

e-Stroke was a major contributor to better diagnosis of brain issues in stroke patients at RBFT. In addition to the speeding up of door-in-door-out and referral times mentioned at the beginning of this chapter, improvements include:

- Patient outcomes, which have seen a significant improvement with initial data indicating a tripling of the rate of those who achieve independence after a major stroke.

- Faster communication and sharing of CT and CTA scan images with other medical teams in the TITAN group, including the ability to view images on hand-held devices and smartphones. This meant that during the pandemic, the hospital was able to maintain the acute care pathway while many consultants were working remotely.

- While working remotely, the implementation of e-Stroke at RBFT meant that the consultants and specialists were not only able to diagnose the impact of stroke on patients, they could also take over the care of patients to free up emergency department doctors to get on with other cases.

In 2023, Health Innovation Oxford and Thames Valley reported that the stroke unit at JRH, a member of TITAN, successfully met an NHS target for the life-changing MT treatment. The treatment can significantly reduce the disabling effects of a stroke on patients and lower the need for long-term care. In 2022, the unit treated 87 patients, achieving a 12 per cent treatment rate – up from just 2 per cent, or 14 patients, in 2019. This represents a sixfold increase in the number of patients receiving this vital treatment. The hospital reached its target with the support of AI systems and the collaborative efforts of TITAN (Health Innovation Oxford and Thames Valley, 2023).

A recent study by stroke physicians, including Dr Kiruba Nagaratnam, highlighted the impact of using AI technology in stroke treatment. The findings revealed that the combination of AI and a collaborative approach significantly accelerated the timely treatment of stroke patients. Notably, the door-in-door-out time was reduced by 49 minutes, and more patients received the critical mechanical thrombectomy when needed (Brainomix, 2024).

Challenges

There was some scepticism among the clinicians about the reliability and the role of AI initially. However, the successful application of the technology in other European centres and the Trust's 'digital by default' vision and objective have helped with adoption of the technology at RBFT. Further trials at RBFT confirmed the effectiveness of the software as a decision-support tool for LVO. However, because of the pandemic, resources were not available to make extensive comparisons with other products on the market. The adoption of e-Stroke Cloud was fast tracked to maintain the care pathway during the COVID-19 pandemic.

After the deployment it became clear that manual upload of images from the scanner to the e-Stroke server could take longer than expected – up to 30 minutes. Something had to be done to reduce the time that it took. Subsequently the implementation team automated the upload. The images are today fed automatically from the scanner to e-Stroke and the upload time has reduced significantly. Analysis of data from December 2020 to January 2021 of head scans conducted manually show:

- 85 CT head scans:
  - average scan to upload time – 34 minutes (range 17 seconds–40 minutes);
  - average processing time – 1 minute 25 seconds.

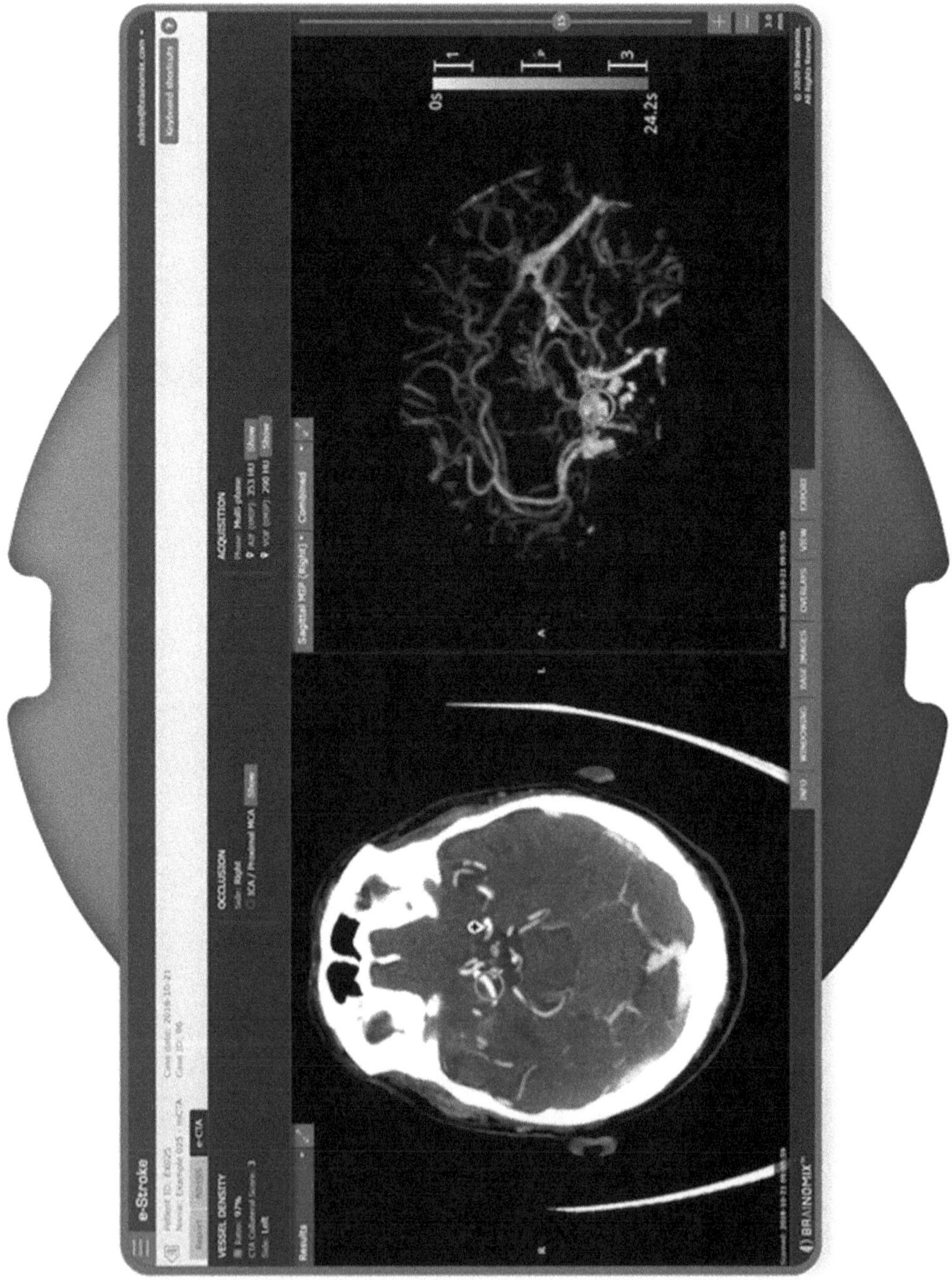

Figure 8.2 An example of stroke damage image analysis provided by e-Stroke

- 42 CT carotid angiograms:
  - average scan to upload time – 23 minutes (range 3–40 minutes);
  - average processing time – 2 minutes.

Analysis of data collected from May to June 2021 after automation of the image upload process:

- 99 CT head scans:
  - average scan to upload time – 7 minutes (range 2–28 minutes);
  - average processing time – 1 minute 26 seconds.
- 59 CT carotid angiograms:
  - average scan to upload time – 8 minutes (range 5–14 minutes);
  - average processing time – 1 minute 21 seconds.

Another challenge is maintaining the AI and ensuring that as new advances and developments in the field of medicine happen, the AI is kept up to date too, that it can work with advances in imaging and diagnosis techniques. This is something that the clinical champion at RBFT is aiming to address over time.

Outlook for the future

This case study has highlighted the use of AI for a particular type of stroke in the front of the brain (anterior circulation). Roughly 20 per cent of patients present with strokes that affect the back of the brain (posterior circulation). Given the success of the current system, we are likely to see demand grow for intelligent decision-support systems for those other types of patients too, leading to future products that can handle more types of strokes.

We are also likely to see requirements for software vendors to show equality and fairness in their AI training; for example, show that the training was done using a sample that included people of all ages, and not limited to certain age groups or ethnicity. This should improve outcomes for all patients.

SUMMARY

This case study provides a great example of the use of AI for good – to enhance clinical outcomes for stroke patients. It shows that doubt and reluctance to embrace new technology can be overcome, and that lengthy procurement processes can be accelerated at times of emergency to ensure the quality of care. The thing that I like about it the most is that the deployment was led by clinicians, domain experts. These specialists wanted to ensure access to good stroke care at any time and anywhere, no matter where and when the patient presented. They are not resting on their laurels either and, despite having faced tough challenges in the pandemic, they are looking to see how else they could use AI to improve their processes further and realise more benefits for patients.

9   USING AI TO OPTIMISE SALES AT WÄRTSILÄ

Symbolic AI or 'good old-fashioned AI' has been around for decades and continues to deliver business value. In this case study I showcase its use in conjunction with constraints inference (see the Glossary at the back of this book for a definition) in a configure price quote (CPQ) system at Wärtsilä where it is used to optimise and partially automate the complicated process of selling engines and other marine and energy products. Some of the company's products, such as generator engines or ship engines, are huge, and are made up of many parts and components. It takes time, effort and expertise to agree all the details with a client in order to produce a quote.

To speed up this process and to reduce lead times, Wärtsilä implemented an intelligent CPQ solution that uses symbolic AI techniques to capture knowledge from experts. This knowledge is then used to guide the specialist sales consultants through the product specification process as they talk the customer through the available options and refine the product configuration. At the end of the process a bill of materials (BoM) is produced from which the product can be priced and a quote prepared.

The introduction of AI in the sales process has significantly reduced the time that it takes to produce quotes for customers, cutting the process time from days to a matter of hours. It has improved the quality of the quotes as they are based on real-time data about components and parts. It has also helped to optimise the sales cycle by efficiently producing the BoM that is then passed on to the engineering teams for product specification and production. Furthermore, it has reduced the time that technical sales consultants spend on preparing quotes, making them available to handle more customer interactions.

ABOUT WÄRTSILÄ

Headquartered in Helsinki, Finland, Wärtsilä is an international supplier of products, solutions and services to the marine and energy sectors with approximately 18,000 employees worldwide. In 2023, Wärtsilä had revenues of €6.01 billion (Wärtsilä Corporation, 2024). It operates in over 200 locations in 80 countries.

The company has been using AI for different business needs for many years. In this case study we focus on the sales optimisation application.

THE BUSINESS CONTEXT

When you buy a new car you are given many options, such as the type of engine, wheels, the material for the seat covers and other trim inside the car. These are complicated enough but you get even more options when buying an engine for a ship or to generate power, for example there will be options for the power rating, fuel type, emissions and maximum speed of the engine. There may be options for the position of the turbocharger and the layout of the exhaust pipes. There may be different types of pumps available and alternatives for air filtration and so on.

These options are linked, for example the position of the turbocharger could exclude some of the options for the size and the layout of the connecting pipes. You could do the configuration manually to create a BoM with hundreds of lines of items and each one in turn made up of smaller parts and components. The process would be lengthy and prone to human error.

THE SALES OPTIMISATION SOLUTION

The sales optimisation solution is the configurator. It is based on an intelligent solution that has a low-code platform for automation of knowledge capture and decision-making. Combined with a database of product information, it captures configuration decisions made by human experts to build the rules and make the constraints trees – tables of valid feature combinations – that it then uses to automate the configuration process for sales optimisation, described above. The trees guide the technical sales consultant through the available options. At each step, the software provides a menu of options, and narrows down the list as the customer makes their choices. The more features of the engine that are decided, the more the choices reduce until the customer gets a configuration that is tailored to their requirements. The output of the process is the BoM that is fed into the quoting system that then generates a quote. The BoM is used to create the product specification that the engineers will use to build the engine as well. It is also used for stock control and ordering the required components.

At Wärtsilä, they have been using AI for sales optimisation for well over a decade. Initially they used a consulting firm to develop the solution but, as time went by, they acquired skills internally and today develop most of the enhancements and any additional requirements in-house. The sales optimisation software is used widely in the division and is maintained by a team of about 10 technical personnel. New product information updates – the knowledge capture – is done in collaboration with subject matter experts. This is ongoing work given that Wärtsilä develops new products, and that components from third parties also change. The solution database of information and the knowledge associated with them have to be updated accordingly. This is all done in-house.

The benefits

In addition to the benefits that have already been highlighted, the configurator helps the internal order processing to ensure supply of the required products and components. It also allows older quotes to be picked up and updated to accommodate customers who have taken a long time to make the decision to buy the product. Sometimes the gap can be as long as a year during which the product designs or the component parts may have changed. With the intelligent configurator, the BoM can be updated easily and a new quote generated.

The overall impact of this is shorter and enhanced customer journeys – an objective that many digitalisation projects aim to achieve. In this case the time that it takes for the customer to interact with a technical sales consultant to specify their requirements is shortened. Additionally, the quality of product specification is improved because the right parts are ordered for the desired engine configuration. The automation reduces delays due to stock issues, for example when the wrong parts are ordered, consequently avoiding both delays in production and customer follow-up calls and support requirements. The improved speed of making a quote and creating the specification through to manufacturing the product has also given the company a competitive edge.

To summarise, the benefits include:

- shorter product configuration and quotation process;
- increased quality and accuracy of the BoM;
- shorter customer journeys from an initial interest in a product to a quote and then an order being placed;
- linking BoMs to product specification and engineering;
- improved internal order processing for parts and components and stock controls;
- easy to update older configurations to supply fresh quotes to clients;
- reduced time to train new technical sales consultants as the solution guides them through the options;
- increased availability of sales personnel.

Challenges

Initially, and unsurprisingly, the implementation team had some learning to do. This was more to do with the approach to knowledge transfer from experts to the solution than anything else. Engines are complex products and capturing information about parts and their dependencies from the expert engineers can be challenging.

The early approach saw product information captured at a detailed level before options at a higher level of decisions were clarified. This led to the solution diving into the details to produce the BoM quickly, which resulted in some errors as not all the constraints at higher levels or branches of the tree had been taken into account. Consequently, following a review, a more top-down approach was taken to produce accurate BoMs. This was over 10 years ago and the solution has been operating reliably ever since.

Then there is the task of managing and maintaining the product information in the database as the company develops new products and responds to new regulatory and environmental requirements. This is an ongoing maintenance requirement rather than a challenge but it has to be factored in when building an intelligent configurator solution.

Figure 9.1 An example of a decision map and the induced decision tree in a PC sale scenario

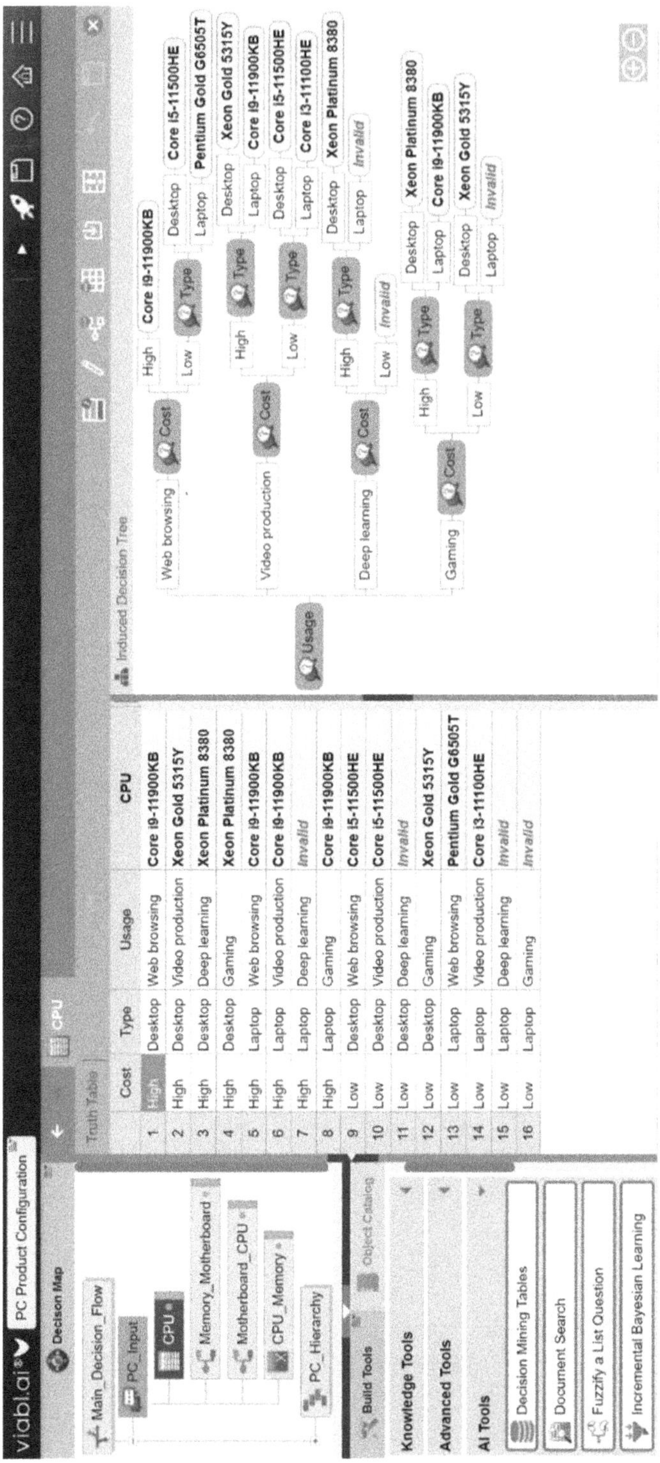

Under the hood of the solution

The CPQ solution uses symbolic AI to capture knowledge from experts to create constraints trees. The knowledge capture is done iteratively; the underlying technology uses machine learning to induce a general decision tree that is then refined with further input from the expert. This includes capturing constraints and the consequences of the decisions resulting in a constraints tree that, combined with a database of product information, is used to guide the technical sales consultant through the process of engine configuration.

The sales consultants use the solution to configure the required features of the product in conversation with the client. As customers make their choices, the configuration is refined with advanced constraints inference from the trees ensuring that only valid features and attributes combinations are selectable. The BoM is produced at the end of the process.

The solution is based on Viabl.ai from XpertRule. The screenshot in Figure 9.1 shows a 'PC Product Configuration' knowledge base opened in the platform's knowledge base editor. The decision map shows the structure of the knowledge base for configuring the central processing unit (CPU) of the PC, while the editor pane (opened for the 'CPU' object) illustrates a truth table that shows all the possible decisions given the inputs, and an automatically induced decision tree generated from the table. This knowledge not only determines the CPU selection but also constrains the user at runtime from picking an invalid combination of values such as 'Cost' = 'Low', 'Type' = 'Laptop', 'Usage' = 'Deep learning' because you need high spec hardware for such a task. The runtime engine combines all these pieces of constraint knowledge to enforce the universal truth.

SUMMARY

Wärtsilä was an early adopter of AI for decision support. This case study has focused on its use of symbolic AI in sales optimisation in its marine and energy business. As a result the company has reduced lead times and can quickly generate quotes for complicated engines that are tailored to the customer's needs and preferences. This gives it a competitive edge as well as other benefits including better product configuration, improved internal ordering and stock control as well as smoother customer journeys.

PART 3
THE SHAPE OF THINGS TO COME:
THE AUTONOMOUS ENTERPRISE

In Part 1 of the book I defined the concept of the autonomous enterprise, and gave an overview of the AI-powered technologies that are making it possible and the important role of these technologies in business innovation and efficiency. In Part 2, I provided a number of case studies showing how AI can be applied in practice, whether in business or in healthcare, to provide both automation and augmentation as a decision-support tool. In Part 3, I focus on the concept of the autonomous enterprise, how we get there, the enablers, and the considerations and actions required of every organisation on their journey to becoming an autonomous enterprise.

10 THE AUTONOMOUS ENTERPRISE

I have established how AI can be used by enterprises for innovation and efficiency with many use case examples provided throughout the early chapters. The case studies demonstrated the value that AI can generate for organisations in real life. The applications were diverse and led to benefits that included more efficient processes, increased flexibility and capacity, augmented decision-making and improved outcomes. The case studies showed that organisations of all sizes can deploy AI and get benefits from it, and do so for many years as shown by the Wärtsilä and Calderdale Council case studies. Their applications of AI have been delivering benefits for well over 10 years and 5 years respectively.

Moreover, the case studies also highlighted that success comes with an open mindset, a willingness to try new ways of doing things, with textbook application of best practice in change management, and with a collaborative approach to introducing new technology, pooling knowledge and sharing resources.

In my view, all the emerging technologies, operational models, trends, best practice and the opportunities for innovation that I have covered in this book are combining to drive us towards the autonomous enterprise. In this chapter I delve into the concept of it, the journey towards it and how organisations can prepare for it.

THE START OF THE JOURNEY

Most organisations have already started their journeys to the autonomous enterprise by automating parts of their processes. In some industries companies are arguably further ahead than others, for example in the automotive industry where many processes have been extensively digitalised and robotised, as seen in car manufacturing processes. Across industries, the trend is for more automation and one indicator is recent investments in technology.

Recent reports show that enterprises' appetite for investment in AI is voracious. For example, *McKinsey Technology Trends Outlook 2024* (Yee et al., 2024) shows that 34 per cent of respondents are either scaling applied AI or have achieved large-scale deployments of it already. Another 39 per cent are either experimenting with it or piloting it, and only a minority of 26 per cent are not investing in it.

The report shows similar levels of adoption for generative AI, with 37 per cent of respondents either scaling up or having achieved large-scale adoption and 38 per cent either experimenting with it or at the stage of piloting it.

Automation changes how things are done in the enterprise. In fact, I would go further and say that it turns the traditional knowledge work inside out. Organisations need to prepare for this and adapt to ensure success. These are the subjects that I explore in the next few sections.

AUTONOMOUS ENTERPRISE DEFINITION

Before we delve deeper into the success factors for the autonomous enterprise, I would like to recap on the definition that I first provided in Chapter 1. The autonomous enterprise:

- Conducts its core daily business functions in a digital and automated manner with minimum human touchpoints, with AI embedded in many of its systems.

- Employs people but they will do fewer repetitive tasks such as checking and settling invoices, and more complex and strategic work, such as handling sensitive and complicated customer cases.

- Not only automates major operations but empowers staff to automate their own repetitive tasks as well. The autonomous enterprise provides IA and augmentation technologies to its staff to help them work more efficiently and productively. It also offers training and support to ensure that they can use those technologies effectively.

- Takes advantage of operational data to create digital twins – virtual models of some of its critical processes – to ensure that work flows through the organisation efficiently and that there are data available to support both automated and human decision-making.

- Gathers process data that it can analyse, so that the autonomous enterprise can learn to improve operations with humans kept in the loop, making it an agile and adaptive enterprise.

- Analyses data to optimise operations, adapt to change, support strategic decisions, enhance risk management, and drive innovation.

Examples of the transactional work that machines do within an autonomous enterprise include:

- data entry;
- checking huge numbers of documents for information;
- cross-referencing and checking data for accuracy;
- answering simple and repetitive enquiries at any helpdesk or during customer interactions;
- finding and capturing information, sourced both internally and externally, to analyse and create business and process intelligence reports;
- assessing cases to process them correctly or to help humans make better decisions;

- generating new assets such as text, images, video, music, and code;
- recording conversations and summarising them with instant translation when needed;
- summarising key points of content like reports and articles, and translating them.

Examples of the higher-value work that people do in an autonomous enterprise include:

- Designing, implementing, overseeing and improving both automated and manual business processes.
- Handling cases or enquiries that are too complex or sensitive for the AI to complete, e.g. bereavement.
- Checking AI automation outputs and ensuring their quality and smooth operations.
- Planning and implementing routines for the AI to capture business intelligence from daily automated operations, and other sources of both internal (e.g. widget sales data) and external data (market trends).
- Acting on the findings of analysis and reporting produced by AI to find opportunities for improving services, products, and marketing and sales to increase revenue, some of this to support decision-making and problem solving in real time. For example if stocks are low in one location, surplus supplies can be found elsewhere in the corporate network of warehouses thanks to analysis of stock data.
- Designing new products and services, planning business growth and geographic expansion and so on. These activities can be augmented with AI, for example hand-drawing 3D visualisation tools for ideation and design concepts.
- Managing the business and operations at team, division and corporate levels.
- Managing relationships with customers, partners and suppliers.

Examples of software tools that empower employees include:

- digital personal assistants that take dictation, arrange meetings and book conference rooms or calls on behalf of the worker;
- AI that transcribes meetings and produces summaries of key points, translates them if necessary and emails them to all stakeholders;
- AI that produces written material or images based on user instructions; for example blurb for brochures, product descriptions, business cases and images for web content;
- intelligent solutions that produce or edit videos;
- AI that provides answers to their questions, for example based on team- or corporate-wide collaboration applications with shared insights and information;
- AI that provides helpdesk and contact centre agents with:
  - best answers based on current and historical information – answers provided in the past to similar questions by their colleagues that have fully and satisfactorily answered customers' questions;

- real-time and in-context signposting to documents that show how similar requirements have been dealt with by the organisation before;

- analysis and reporting for decision support;

- automated work pattern insights and advice that can improve work–life balance for employees by optimising workloads and their fair distribution among team members, while increasing productivity;

- help with low- or no-code automation software to allow them to automate their repetitive tasks, provided together with training, hand-holding, governance and guiding frameworks.

Behind the definition that I have provided lie a whole series of good practices without which the autonomous enterprise would not be possible. I explore these later on in this chapter.

Another thing to note is that for new ventures it is easy to start out as an autonomous enterprise, with the latest automation technologies deployed from the beginning. Examples of this include Lemonade, the US-based insurance company that was set up from the start to run highly automated operations. It is not so easy to become an autonomous enterprise for established businesses with a mix of old and new systems.

It is not about ripping out old systems and replacing them with new ones in established organisations either. For them there is a journey towards autonomy and that means incrementally automating suitable processes over a period of several years.

TURNING KNOWLEDGE PROCESSES INSIDE OUT

Knowledge work in organisations today is mostly conducted in a semi-automated fashion. There are software solutions such as ERP and line of business applications that bring a lot of business information together for knowledge workers to do their work. These include some automated information updates and calculations, and increasingly smart help tools and best answers. In organisations, there are pools of people sitting in offices and using these solutions to do their jobs. The autonomous enterprise will change this model in that there will be pools of software on servers running in the cloud handling high-volume business transactions with people looking after them, guiding them or handling the exceptions that the machines cannot deal with. This is highlighted in Figure 10.1.

The change in the model of knowledge work will mean that enterprises will have to document not only processes but the expertise that they codify to create the automations. Maintaining the knowledge will be critical to allow processes to be conducted manually should a system failure happen, and to monitor the accuracy and efficiency of the codified operations. This is very important as with low-code development environments, experts can program their knowledge into software robots to create new automations and then move on to other jobs, leaving the organisation without the knowledge of how things are done except for the coding of the robot. With AI-powered automation, the AI might develop new ways of doing things and if not adequately supervised by humans, the enterprise might become incapable of following what the AI is doing and be unable to take risk mitigating action or deal with any issues that arise from the changes.

Organisations will have to document their processes with full version control and life-cycle management to ensure that change can be managed along with the source code of their intelligent automations. Enterprises have to be able to roll back a version of an automated process if a problem is encountered when it goes live.

Figure 10.1 Inside-out knowledge work in the autonomous enterprise

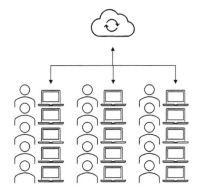

Today's knowledge workers conduct business processes on their PCs using software on servers in the cloud

Tomorrow's autonomous enterprise knowledge workers will supervise automation software robots and automated processes running on servers in the cloud and handle breakdowns and exceptions, as well as improve and update the automations

It will be necessary to increase auditing and monitoring of operations to ensure that processes are run correctly and that they comply with corporate policies and standards, and regulatory and ethical requirements, such as the EU's new AI Act.

Training and knowledge transfer will have to be carefully managed for leavers and joiners and for succession planning and team career advancements. The managers of the future will mostly come from this pool of trained personnel and should gain good knowledge of how things are done as they come through the ranks.

Even some of these requirements can be automated, for example there are already technologies out there, such as process and task mining covered in Chapter 5, that capture process information and document it. Document management and software version and life-cycle control solutions have been around for decades.

The upshot of all of this is that we need to think about the transformation to autonomous enterprise and its impact on how we do things.

In the next sections I explore some of the characteristics of autonomous enterprises.

THE AUTONOMOUS ENTERPRISE MINDSET

While some organisations are very risk averse and avoid adopting new technologies, others embrace them. One example is Siemens GBS, which was the subject of the case study in Chapter 6. Although the case study was about its Bionic Agent, the company has been at the forefront of adopting advanced technology in many different ways, including the use of IA. Its leadership is happy to have new solutions trialled and with each one the organisation gains more skills and experiences.

The current wave of autonomous enterprises has emerged from this kind of mindset: organisations led by technology champions who are willing to try new ways of doing things. In this approach to adopting new technology, as in any others, it is important to manage the associated risks and capture the lessons learnt to feed into future projects.

The autonomous enterprises that emerge from new ventures, those that bet big on intelligent technology from the start, will have the kind of mindset that will have moved well beyond concepts of recent decades such as digital- or automated-first. For them, automation is the norm.

The autonomous enterprise mindset ensures that, while core business functions are automated as a strategic approach, the staff at all levels of the organisation are empowered to use technology to automate their own less interesting and transactional tasks. With the addition of process intelligence captured through process or task mining applications, staff are enabled to check their own performance and make informed decisions about their work habits to improve it. The organisation supports them by providing the technology, the training and the hand-holding that staff need to do this.

Starting with the end in mind

Adoption of AI should not be about having the latest new shiny thing but to achieve specific outcomes. In the Calderdale Council case study in Chapter 7 we saw clearly that the council started with the end in mind. The project was to improve customer services and to create capacity. Implementing VIRA, the IVA, was just one part of the bigger digitalisation project that saw an overhaul of the website and the introduction of smart forms. These work together well because they were all part of achieving a clear objective of increasing customer self-service with more digitalisation of services.

The joined-up, collaborative approach with pooling of resources

The benefits of a joined-up approach were demonstrated by the RBFT case study in Chapter 8, as well as the Calderdale Council VIRA implementation. The deployment of the intelligent e-Stroke Suite was part of a bigger review of the complete stroke care system.

Joined-up working involves collaboration with different teams, which can be inside or outside the organisation. In the RBFT case study the adoption of the intelligent e-Stroke system was done collaboratively with a number of hospitals involved in the TITAN group. It demonstrated how knowledge and CT scan data, shared among the members of the group, increased access to specialists and improved patient outcomes.

In the Siemens GBS case study we learnt that the organisation has a dedicated team that provides technology design and development services to its other departments. This helps it to keep skills in-house to develop new technology solutions as required. Another aspect of the development of the Bionic Agent was the organisation's desire to make it reusable. It designed the solution so that it could be repurposed and used for other requirements in the future. Accordingly, the organisation captured and curated technology knowledge and know-how for reuse in the future.

The theme of resource pooling was repeated in the Wärtsilä case study. The company reduced its reliance on external consultancies by developing skills internally and creating a team that handles the development and maintenance of its intelligent CPQ solutions in-house.

Focus on phygital

The joined-up approach is particularly important when we look to joining up the digital and physical worlds. This was illustrated by the Wärtsilä case study where the automatically generated bill of materials went from the virtual world of the CPQ system to the real world of component stores and their stock levels, and to the engineering team who would get the components together in order to build the product that was ordered. Another example that illustrates why thinking phygital is important is car insurance. The easiest way to automate this is by providing quotes based on automated and intelligent risk assessments, and then accepting payments and processing the insurance policies, all of it done online. In phygital the process can go further, for example if someone opts to have a car black box installed to get a reduced premium. While 90 per cent of the process of insuring the car could be automated, at some point there will need to be a handover to someone who is charged with sending the black box to the client and arranging for it to be installed in their car. In a joined-up approach, the impact of automating the rest of the processes on the manual part would be assessed, risks such as black box supply and demand fluctuations taken into account and information about the state of risks shared with the intelligent solution that is involved in providing the quote. The system can then make decisions about the availability of the offer and inform the customer accordingly.

In contrast, in a disjointed approach, the customer would be offered cover at a discounted premium but the company might not be able to dispatch the black box for weeks due to supply issues, thus depriving itself of valuable driver data for insurance purposes.

Good data stewardship

Another aspect of joined-up work and essential for automation is good data management. Good practice is essential, and with the help of intelligent technology, organisations can take analysis for decision support to new levels. In terms of good practice, we saw in the Calderdale case study in Chapter 7 that the council made extensive use of the data that it had from past chat conversations to train and enhance VIRA. It also gathered user feedback and captured operational data to monitor the performance of VIRA and to measure the quality of the customer experiences – it checked at what points customers dropped off, to get insights into what needed improving.

In the RBFT case study we saw another aspect of data stewardship: ensuring that the sharing of data with external partners was within data privacy requirements. With anonymised patient identifiers used, the names of the patients were not visible in the shared scan images.

Good data stewardship is essential for AI and business automation. Today, organisations have data in hundreds of business systems on premises and on cloud. The data have to be maintained, their quality assured and updates propagated across systems to synchronise changes and ensure that operations run smoothly. Good data stewardship ensures that the organisation has a complete and accurate view of its key data, its golden records, such as customer and product data. Investment in data integration and quality assurance solutions is essential. These technologies are advancing fast, and today it is possible to integrate swathes of business data to feed cognitive systems that can make automated predictions to advise decision-makers or make decisions automatically and execute processes accordingly. Some of the biggest companies, such as one of the largest consumer packaged goods manufacturers in the world, is already using these types of systems.

Data-driven insights and innovation

The industry has been talking about analytics for decision support for decades. Machine learning is taking this capability to new levels, enabling more automated decision-making and process execution. Intelligent analytics enable budding autonomous enterprises to capture business critical data and apply analytics to get business and operational insights rapidly.

In Chapter 1 we learnt how Ocado, the UK online grocery store, conducts millions of demand and supply forecasts a day to ensure the freshness of its stock to minimise food waste. In its 2023 annual report (Ocado Group, 2023) the company stated that it had improved its food waste from 0.9 per cent of its sales in the previous 12 months to 0.7 per cent. This is a double saving of costs and food waste.

In Chapter 4 we learnt how AI can help enterprises find the opportunity in a mass of data to improve something: one example is to use deep learning to run advanced analytics to gain insights on how your company is perceived by its customers. The analysis can provide insights over large populations or over long periods of time, to detect the likelihood of customers defecting to a competitor or defaulting on invoice payments. This would allow the organisation to make special offers to the clients or prepare to offer them a payment plan should it become necessary. Another opportunity is to analyse customer feedback on white goods and other products, either directly or by understanding the sentiment from comments posted on social media and to feed that information back to product engineering teams for enhancements.

Agility

Benjamin Franklin once said, 'In this world nothing can be said to be certain, except death and taxes.' I would add change to this list. Our world changes all the time, be it ecologically, environmentally, politically, socially or technologically. The latter faster than most of us can keep up with.

Change means that demand for products and services shifts. This changing pattern leads to some products and services having to be retired and new ones developed and brought to market. Businesses need agility to be able to move with the times, and that ability is powered by data and information, for example where the issues and bottlenecks are in their organisations or what to change in response to new requirements. Data captured from automated operations can provide these insights. We saw a great example of this in the Calderdale Council case study where the contact centre staff were trained to add new vocabulary to VIRA and teach it to deal with conversations in new contexts so that the council could answer additional customer questions. Over the COVID-19 pandemic this capability helped the organisation to deal with changes that the UK Government mandated, often at short notice, many relating to new rules for lockdowns, self-testing and isolation, in schools, in social care and more. This is agility in practice, an important facet of the autonomous enterprise.

It is also important to keep an eye on emerging technology and global trends to prepare for the longer term. It helps to always keep aspirations going and to visualise the shape of things to come: how emerging technological developments might impact the organisation, and what it would need to do to be ready for that future.

THE ONGOING AUTONOMOUS ENTERPRISE JOURNEY

While many organisations have already automated some of their business processes and operations, new developments will bring fresh opportunities for innovation. Take the automotive industry: car manufacturing processes have been highly automated with robots assembling car parts to create specific models and customised versions of cars to order. The robots receive their instructions from microchips that have been preloaded with the build data or they get the information downloaded to them.

Customers can choose the car configuration that they want when they order the car, and these days most of the configuration work is done on a self-service basis. Intelligent CPQ solutions take the customers through an array of options such as engine type, wheels, interior materials and trims, information and entertainment systems and so on. The choices are captured and used to create the product specification that is sent to manufacturing – loaded onto a chip for a largely automated manufacturing process to get started.

But what if it became possible to take the automation further, for example allowing the finished car to be automatically loaded onto a truck for delivery to the customer? What if the lorry could be replaced by an autonomous one to drive and deliver the car to the customer at home? What if the car itself was autonomous and could actually drive itself to the customer's house? This would bring benefits to the manufacturer, the customer and the environment. It would mean:

- The customer doesn't have to make a journey to the showroom to pick up the car, cutting out the associated energy consumption and carbon emissions from power generation for travelling there.
- It would not be necessary to buy a forklift or a ramp or a robot for loading the car onto a lorry, reducing investment requirements in machinery, cutting demand and reducing their manufacture and associated industrial waste.

- A lorry, be it manual or autonomous, would not be required to deliver the car to the customer, consequently reducing demand for lorries and the industrial waste that their manufacturing produces.

Figure 10.2 provides an overview of car buying scenarios today and in future.

These kinds of scenarios are closer to becoming reality than we think; there are already giant robots that park cars in car parks with great accuracy. Some load the cars onto a car-sized platform on wheels using a forklift truck mechanism before depositing them in parking bays. There are also trials of autonomous vehicles going on in many cities around the world: for example autonomous taxis in San Francisco.

The point that I am making here is that, no matter in what industry you operate, even in the highly automated automotive industry, there will be other opportunities for automation that will become possible. This is about thinking of possibilities and innovating, with the people in the organisation continuously monitoring emerging technology trends to provide the ideas, the planning and the development of the next leading-edge capability.

HOW THINGS CAN GO WRONG

There are many organisations that have introduced automation in parts of their operations but in a disjointed way that can create problems for both the company and its customers. For example, can you imagine the hurt that a customer would feel if tickets to a much anticipated gig by a favourite band that they had booked as part of a phygital marketing offer never materialised? It would take an awful lot of time and grovelling to the customer by the company to make up for that kind of let-down.

There is much more that can go wrong, from simply badly designed online user interfaces to inadequate integration between systems that prevent employees doing their jobs well. I examine some of these factors in this section. These are well-known issues by veterans of the IT industry because they cause problems for organisations today. They would do so for autonomous enterprises of the future as well if not addressed.

Old and disjointed systems

One of the biggest problems in enterprises stems from their lack of investment in technology modernisation. Systems need to be kept up to date and their lifetimes managed so that over time they can be replaced with new ones with better features and connections to other systems. The lack of investment results in organisations relying on old and bloated systems – full of out-of-date data – that make it hard for employees to do their work. Problems faced by staff include not being able to find the correct customer record because of duplicated records, or incomplete product information that is out of sync with the latest models and offerings, as well as outdated information about the customer and their purchase history. Duplicate and outdated data would cause problems, with AI either passing on a case to a human as an exception or making errors. It would completely defeat the objective of automating processes to improve throughput and efficiency. These types of problems lead to a lack of job satisfaction among staff as well and increased attrition rates.

Figure 10.2 Car buying processes today and possibilities for automation in future

Scenario 1: The customer orders a car online and customises it to their liking. The car is manufactured and taken to a show room where the customer picks it up and drives it away.

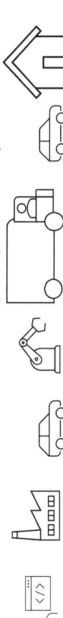

Scenario 2: The customer orders a car online and customises it to their liking. The car is manufactured and is manually loaded to a lorry, driven by a driver who delivers the car to the customer's home.

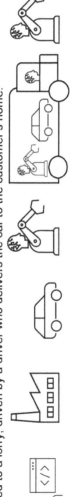

Scenario 3: The customer orders a car online and customises it to their liking. The car is manufactured and loaded by a robot to an autonomous lorry that delivers the car to the customer's home.

Scenario 4: The customer orders a car online and customises it to their liking. The car is manufactured and autonomously drives itself to the customer's home. This scenario optimises the car delivery model by reducing journeys and cutting out the need to invest in forklifts and lorries.

Outdated software systems that are no longer supported by their manufacturers can be cybersecurity hazards because vendors typically enhance their software security in the updates that they release. Older systems leave known vulnerabilities open to use by hackers.

Poor data integration

Older systems are difficult to integrate with other systems and, as a consequence, data cannot easily be maintained and synchronised between them. This results in problems such as out-of-date customer and product information, making it hard for the company to deliver its services and deal with customer enquiries smoothly whether the process is automated or not. Poor-quality data lead to more problems, for instance, mistakes when undertaking business processes. If you automate a process with poor data then, as the speed of processing increases, the data problem is propagated through to more transactions and to more systems, with chaos ensuing.

Poor customer experience

We have all experienced poorly designed websites and apps – those that leave us going round and round from page to page on websites but never finding the information that we are looking for. The same thing can happen with chatbots or IVAs that are poorly trained with limited understanding of the subject matter that they are supposed to be able to handle. Similarly, phone switchboard options can take you through many topics except the one that you are looking for, and then a recorded voice may well advise you to visit the website and hang up on you. These are badly designed customer journeys. They have been created without the customer perspective leading to unnecessary contact by phone and other channels. These types of issues lead to much customer dissatisfaction.

Inadequate staff training

Another problem is implementing highly advanced systems but failing to adequately train staff to use them. This means that some staff will find it difficult to do their work and some will even try to bypass the system. There are examples of this where, instead of putting all of the information into the provided system, members of a team enter some of it into spreadsheets for their personal use. The spreadsheets are not shared and leave other staff in the team in the dark about the cases that their colleagues have been working on. This means that team members cannot answer any questions about the case work and are not able to address any issues that might arise when those colleagues are not in the office.

This kind of practice leads to a growing problem of 'shadow IT', which is when employees use software applications outside recommended practices and IT policies, including accessing unapproved apps remotely on cloud. As well as limiting collaboration, the reduced levels of visibility and auditability of process steps and decisions can lead to risks such as failure to comply with regulatory requirements and information quality and security issues.

In a contact centre, this type of scenario would mean that staff are not able to use the systems that are there to provide the information that they need to answer customers' questions. Imagine being on the phone to an unhappy client and not being able to use the system that would allow you to help them. As the agent, you would get more and more flustered, and to keep the customer happy, you might make them a special offer that you cannot provide, leading to further customer dissatisfaction.

MY PERSONAL EXPERIENCE OF HOW THINGS CAN GO WRONG

Without a joined-up approach, and use of automation in this data-heavy phygital world, things can go very wrong. An example of a scenario to be avoided is the terrible experience that I had a few years ago when I contacted my mobile phone operator to upgrade my plan. The company in question has since fixed the problems that I describe next, but because of my experience, I will always think of them as a shambolic organisation. This is exactly the sort of damage to reputation that companies must mitigate through good customer service.

I had three existing devices supplied to me by the company, only one of which was a phone with a number that I was familiar with. Unbeknown to me, the company allocated phone numbers to the other two devices as well, even though they were not mobile phones. With similar pricing and usage patterns, it was not possible for me to identify which was which on my phone bills either. When I called to discuss upgrade options with the phone operator, I found that the contact centre agent could not tell me which phone number was allocated to which device either. There was no information on her system that linked the phone number to the device type – phone, dongle, tablet and so on. That made the upgrade discussion difficult because she expected me to give her information that the company had not supplied.

She did not have easy access to the latest product stock information either and took several minutes to check the relevant databases. Having finally checked the product portfolio and stock databases, she told me that the model of the phone that I wanted was not available but she would send me the next model up on a complimentary basis. She also said that she would send me two new SIM cards, one for my phone and one for one of the other devices that I was also upgrading. The instruction that I got was that once I received the SIM cards I should go on the website and activate each SIM. When I asked her how to do this she told me that I had to put the phone number for each device in the activation field of the SIM web page. I explained to her that the second device was not a phone and I did not know its phone number but she could not help me with that.

Needless to say that a painful sequence of activating SIMs by trial and error followed that went on for several days, leading to a number of replacement SIM cards having to be dispatched to me, my third device getting disconnected unnecessarily and having to be reconnected with a new SIM card. It was a long and painful customer journey for me, having to make many calls to the phone company, put up with their long waiting times and listen to the painful music that they played while I waited on the phone. Each call was picked up by a different agent who had similar issues:

- They had poor data:

  - The information that I had been given by the operator about the products that I had was incomplete.

  - The way that the data had been stored was inadequate, that is, the phone numbers that were stored in my records did not show the types of devices that I had.

  - The product catalogue was out of date – at first, it showed that the model that I wanted was out of stock, but later someone in the organisation managed to find one and send it to me.

- Poor system performance:

  - Either their databases were slow to respond, leaving the agents and me waiting for minutes on live calls;

  - or they had not provided sufficient training to their staff to enable them to use the systems to get the information that they needed to answer their customers' questions.

- Disjointed automation:

  - While some aspects of the service were partially automated, for example SIM activation, the rest of the processes were manual and disjointed. Clearly there were no links between customer information, product catalogues, stocks and the information needed for SIM activation.

- The operations led to staff dissatisfaction:

  - This disjointed set of phone, online and manual steps made the service wholly inadequate, leading not just to customer dissatisfaction but to feelings of anxiety and frustration by staff.

  - Even their customer complaint team could not raise much enthusiasm to deal with the complaint that I made following my horrible experience. Clearly I was one of many dissatisfied customers they had had that day. There were no follow-ups.

When my new phone arrived, I discovered that it was the model that I had asked for originally and not the complimentary upgrade to the next best product that I had been promised. I had received no communication about this and felt seriously let down by the company.

They failed to notify me of the change in the model that they supplied me – basically the special offer that the contact centre agent had made me could not be fulfilled, and no explanation was offered as to why. This completely negated the goodwill that they had shown when the agent made me the offer of a better model.

This company had significant information problems, but many of these could have been resolved by automation:

- product catalogue and stock levels updated automatically in real time, and the information uploaded to a system that the contact centre agents had access to and that worked fast in real time;

- product types added as a field to the database of phone numbers that were used for device identification;

- notifications of changes to orders sent automatically.

There is really no excuse for this kind of poor service, even if an organisation is full of legacy systems that are difficult to upgrade and integrate. Leading companies have shown that the use of IA technologies such as RPA with IDP can fill the integration gap between systems, help with process automation and ensure data accuracy and quality.

In the case of my mobile phone operator, an apology for poor service should have been sent automatically as well but there were no apologies and no follow-ups.

When AI Goes Wrong

In the next chapter I provide examples of when AI goes wrong, including a chatbot that learnt bad language from its online environment. In Chapter 3 I discussed how generative AI can hallucinate and make errors. When AI goes wrong live in production, the scale of the resulting problems can be very big, and that is why it is advisable to have humans check its output for accuracy, quality, relevance, compliance with corporate policies and regulatory requirements, and ethical processing of information and cases. Humans should also ensure that AI does not change its behaviour in a way that negatively affects the service it provides, for example in its pursuit of efficiency, develop a style of communication that humans cannot understand.

SUMMARY

In this chapter I covered the autonomous enterprise in detail and described the factors that help organisations with their journeys to becoming one. I highlighted the need for joined-up and well thought-out automation that provides good experiences for both customers and staff. The journey will be never-ending as new technologies emerge and enable us to do more. I highlighted this in the car manufacturing scenario to show how even an advanced industry in terms of enterprise autonomy cannot stand still.

Finally, I looked at how things can go wrong and the factors that contribute to it, including legacy systems, poor system integration, out-of-date information and inadequate training of staff. I shared my first-hand experience of poor service by a mobile phone operator that I believe was caused by all of these factors.

In the next chapter I discuss the future of jobs and the ethics of technology.

11 AUTOMATION AND SOCIETY

In this chapter I look at the impact of automation on employment in the past and extrapolate to suggest the likely impact in the future. This discussion about jobs leads to a more general discussion about ethics and the way that AI can be applied for the good of society.

JOBS FOR HUMANS

The elephant in the room is the question of jobs for humans. What is going to be the impact of automation of work on the jobs landscape and society as a whole? These are complex questions that cannot be answered easily, given that in the jobs market there are other factors at work.

While the jobs market varies by country, we can gain some insights by looking at the statistics in the UK. Firstly, nearly one-fifth (18 per cent) of the population is over 65 (Centre for Aging Better, 2024)) The effect of the ageing population is showing in rising vacancies for jobs such as healthcare professionals. There are not enough young people coming through to take up the vacancies as people in the existing workforce leave the sector either to change careers or to retire. According to the UK government job site, https://findajob.dwp.gov.uk/, there were 20,321 vacancies in healthcare in the UK at the time of writing. This is leading to serious problems for the National Health Service, affecting availability of treatments and in turn health and well-being in the country. It is causing inactivity, with untreated conditions affecting the workforce, as those who are waiting for treatment often have to take sick leave or give up work altogether.

Macro factors also impact the market. For example, job vacancies in the UK dropped and unemployment went up in 2020, early in the pandemic, but because of Brexit and COVID-19, many EU workers left the country. The result was a gaping hole in skills in some sectors in the UK including healthcare and veterinary medicine, agriculture, hospitality and tourism, construction and transport.

In June 2021, a UK Government study revealed that vacancies were becoming harder to fill due to a lack of qualifications, relevant skills, or experience, as shown in Figure 11.1 (UK Government, 2020).

In 2019, nearly a quarter of all job vacancies (24 per cent) were due to skill shortages, up from 22 per cent in the 2013–2017 period. The highest rates of skill shortages were in construction and manufacturing, both at 36 per cent. In construction, this was the same as in 2017, while in manufacturing, it increased from 29 per cent in 2017.

Figure 11.1 Number and density of skill-shortage vacancies (SSVs), by sector (Source: UK Government, 2020)

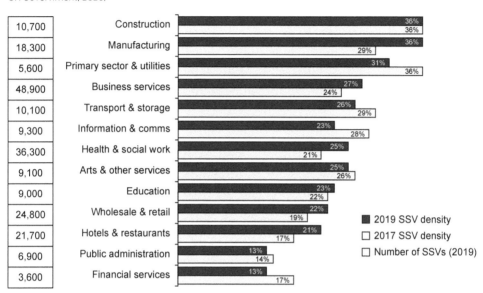

Number of SSVs (2019)	Sector	2019 SSV density	2017 SSV density
10,700	Construction	36%	36%
18,300	Manufacturing	36%	29%
5,600	Primary sector & utilities	31%	36%
48,900	Business services	27%	24%
10,100	Transport & storage	26%	29%
9,300	Information & comms	23%	28%
36,300	Health & social work	25%	21%
9,100	Arts & other services	25%	26%
9,000	Education	23%	22%
24,800	Wholesale & retail	22%	19%
21,700	Hotels & restaurants	21%	17%
6,900	Public administration	13%	14%
3,600	Financial services	13%	17%

Legend: ■ 2019 SSV density □ 2017 SSV density □ Number of SSVs (2019)

Base: All establishment vacancies (range: public admin. & retail 3,584)

At the same time, in 2019, the Office for National Statistics (ONS) in the UK conducted a study, 'Which occupations are at highest risk of being automated?' (ONS, 2019), which estimated that 7.4 per cent of jobs were at high risk of being lost due to automation. The estimate had dropped from 8.1 per cent to 7.4 per cent between 2011 and 2017. The agency surmised that the need for skills for more complex jobs had increased over this period and these were jobs that were more difficult to automate.

The implication of these studies is unsurprising: skills are very much in demand and skilled jobs have a low likelihood of being automated. The picture may very well change because of the impact of generative AI and other advances in AI. However, I believe human skills will remain essential, as many job aspects still require human decision-making and expertise. Two examples illustrate this point: one from a German teacher in a secondary school in England, and the other from a professional translator. Both have noted that the quality of automated translations that they have seen does not yet match human-translated work. Moreover, the professional translator emphasised the difficulties a robot might face when translating books, for instance when dealing with humour or feelings, and in particular with dialects or regional accents; for example in *Lady Chatterley's Lover* by D. H. Lawrence the gamekeeper speaks English with a Derbyshire accent. Translating these nuances requires human common sense and cultural awareness, which AI currently lacks. AI systems are not yet trained in the various dialects and accents used around the world, making accurate translations challenging.

Similarly, my experience with generative AI has shown me that it requires skilled input to produce correct and relevant output. I believe that skilled professionals will benefit from generative AI, as it serves as an assistant to enhance their work rather than replace them. This symbiotic relationship between humans and AI will likely continue until further significant advances are made in AI development.

This need for skilled workers will likely continue to provide opportunities for human work, although there may be fewer jobs than before. The overall reduction in jobs is expected because AI can augment human capabilities, allowing us to complete tasks more quickly. For example, with AI assistance, a task that once took a full day might now be completed in half the time. This increased productivity reduces the need for additional staff.

However, this reduction in the number of jobs may be balanced by the rising number of people retiring due to ageing. It is not just the fact that older people will be leaving the workforce but also that they will require care and support which will create jobs balancing some of those that are lost due to AI automation. There will be additional jobs created as well, for example roles for people to look after all the automations that we will be creating in the coming years.

The nature of the skills required will change too to cater for the demands of an increasingly technology-based economy: for example people to design, develop and maintain new smart products, experiences and services. Clearly measures are needed by governments and industries to help people get the skills that are in demand, not only to fill current vacancies but to help maintain employment against the backdrop of increasing automation. The more opportunities we create for people to develop skills that are in demand, the better we mitigate risks of increasing unemployment because of automation.

This brings me to the topic of the changing jobs landscape. We should not limit the conversation to existing jobs, because throughout history we have seen new jobs being created while others have disappeared. I cover this in more detail next.

CREATION OF NEW ROLES

In addition to the current skills shortage, another factor to consider is the creation of new jobs. If you look back at history, many different kinds of jobs emerged and then disappeared due to automation or changes in lifestyles. White goods, for example, have automated our home chores to a large degree, reducing the need for domestic staff. Farming has been mechanised and automated significantly, reducing the need for hundreds of farm workers. We can see the trend for mechanisation and digitalisation of work continuing in many different industries, such as:

- Banking:
  - Automated teller machines started to appear in the late 1970s reducing the need for people to go inside bank branches to get cash.
  - Increased levels of self-service such as app-based banking services have almost entirely eliminated the need for most of us to visit bank branches in person.

- Manufacturing:
  - Robots have been building cars in factories for decades.
- Retail:
  - The use of robots in warehouses to pick and pack groceries and other products is becoming widespread, fuelled by demand for online shopping.
- Air travel:
  - Self-service passenger and baggage check-in at airports has become widely available with typically only a few staffed kiosks available to handle self-check-in issues or check in any passengers that prefer to do it in person.

These automations that have developed in the past 50 years are only a few examples of the bigger picture of increased uses of computers and digitalisation of business processes and self-service using online channels. The increasing levels of computerisation and automation of work have not led to mass unemployment for humans to date, and all the while the world population has increased dramatically. Unemployment data from the UK and US provide interesting insights. Firstly, data from the ONS on vacancies and unemployment (Office for National Statistics, 2024) show employment rates in the UK today are at similar levels to 23 years ago in the early 2000s, having gone through waves of change in between due to economic recessions and technological advancements. The number of vacancies, having peaked in 2022, has dropped in the last 18 months but is still higher than it was in 2001. These insights are highlighted in Figure 11.2.

Figure 11.2 UK unemployment versus vacancies (Source: ONS, 2024)

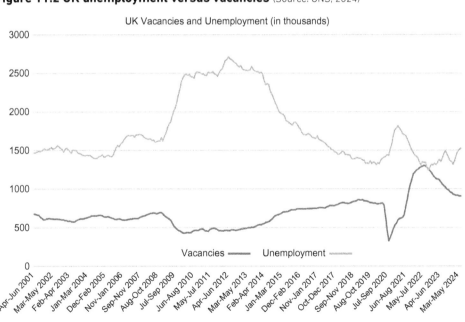

Secondly, the US unemployment figures compiled by the US Bureau of Labor Statistics (2024) tell a similar story. They show the impact of the pandemic but that the rate has returned to a pre-pandemic level but is lower than 20 years ago in 2004, as shown in Figure 11.3.

Figure 11.3 US civilian unemployment rate, seasonally adjusted (the shaded area represents recession, as determined by the US National Bureau of Economic Research)

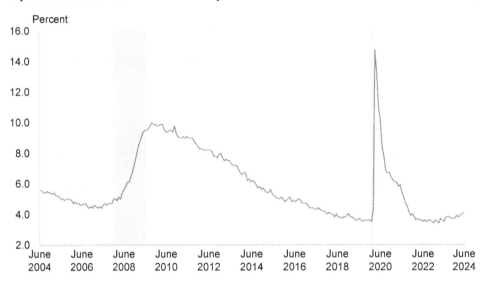

I believe one reason for today's low unemployment rate, despite existing levels of computerisation and automation of office work, is that new jobs have been created – and it is likely that they will continue to be created as seen over past centuries. New jobs in recent times have included social media marketing roles, industry research and analysis, drone pilots, and building energy assessors and certifiers. Vacancies in sectors like delivery and warehousing have skyrocketed. This surge is driven by a confluence of factors: changing lifestyles and work models due to the pandemic, increased technology use and political developments such as Brexit. Accordingly, new jobs and growing employment in some sectors are likely to offset job losses due to AI-enabled automation of knowledge work. Examples of where new roles are likely to be created include: the environment sector where demand for skills is likely to go up as we search for new solutions and services to help mitigate risks and the impact of global warming; and the space race, which is hotting up with demand for skills to take the human race to other planets for research as well as for future commerce and tourism. This is likely to lead to more skilled work opportunities albeit in small numbers, but it is an indication of how new jobs will be created with advances in science and technology.

AI will augment many of the jobs mentioned above and help by boosting analysis of data and identification of potential solutions. It is important to note that, because AI leads to more changes in our work and lifestyles and creates new models for business, it is likely to create new jobs itself (and in fact it has been doing so with roles such as AI supervisors and data scientists):

- In the technology sector, we will need more skills to design and build all the technology, machines and robots that we are likely to need, to maintain them and manage their life cycles.

- Skills in technology will need to be complemented by design and artistic creativity to create compelling experiences for the users of AI-powered solutions. This will increase demand for creative people and is a line of business that we are likely to see grow, following in the footsteps of the digital revolution that gave rise to many digital design agencies.

- With technology playing a big part in many aspects of life and work, the workforce of the future will need to be highly tech-savvy. We will need more technology teachers and lecturers to educate and train the workforce of the future, and to aid self-learning by creating new online courses to close the skills gap.

- AI also brings great opportunities for innovation, as mentioned in Chapter 4. The opportunities cover many different walks of life, from music and arts to hospitality, transport, business services and heavy industries. The opportunities for entrepreneurship are huge and are likely to lead to a variety of new roles and vacancies.

AI ETHICS

Another important topic in the age of automation is the ethics of AI. There have been many examples of AI either developing bad behaviour or showing bias, for example Microsoft's Tay (Griffin, 2016) which learnt bad behaviour from Twitter conversations and had to be shut down after it made offensive tweets. As another example, some facial recognition software was found to be poor at correctly recognising women and that led to some women, including myself, having problems with banking apps where automated identity checks were required.

Problems with AI can happen in many different ways, including:

- Poor design and enhancement decisions – this could lead to substandard interfaces that can deprive some users of being able to use the product, or build exclusion or prejudicial bias into the software.

- Inadequate training data that are not representative of the population that it is targeting, for example not enough samples of women's faces to train AI for facial recognition. This can lead to errors or biased decisions automatically made by AI when it goes live.

- Inadequate testing against a wide variety of use cases and user scenarios, consequently not effectively mitigating risks.

- Opaque decision-making by AI that cannot be explained – this is leading to demand for explainable AI that is necessary to show fairness and compliance with regulatory requirements, for example in healthcare and financial services. Vendors are working on addressing this type of issue, for example I know one NLP vendor that allows the user to trace decisions made by the software to the training that the AI received so that issues can become visible and be addressed.

- No shades of grey decision-making: When it comes to decision-making, humans can interpret rules and apply common sense to cases where there are no clear-cut answers. With machines making rules-based decisions, there is likely to be an increase in inexplicable decisions, like a mortgage application being turned down for minor reasons or the system setting some tough conditions for agreeing to a mortgage, like setting dates by which some survey-related issues have to be resolved before the mortgage application is approved. In financial services, many countries require humans to review automated decisions and approve them, and clear guidance will be needed for them to deal with situations when the machine says no.

- Sounding totally believable and yet wrong: Generative AI can sound extremely believable and authoritative in its answers to questions and yet it can be hallucinating and wrong. This scenario could lead to problems for people if they accept its answers without checking their accuracy. In fact the analyst firm Gartner (Fisher, 2024) has predicted that before long, generative AI will lead to the death of a customer, in such a scenario.

In the wrong hands AI can be used maliciously for many purposes, from cybercrime to controlling human lives.

A report titled *The Malicious Use of Artificial Intelligence: Forecasting, Prevention, and Mitigation* (Brundage et al., 2018), written by a group of experts from different academic and research institutes including the universities of Oxford and Cambridge and the OpenAI foundation, explores the potential risks of malicious AI in great detail and calls for prevention and risk mitigation.

The report identifies risks such as AI making it easier for bad actors to undertake more automated and highly targeted cybercrime, or create new types of attacks that explore the vulnerabilities of AI systems, for example where they rely on human speech synthesis and the risks of impersonation. Other risks include AI used for autonomous weapons and political surveillance. The report challenges policymakers to collaborate with the technology industry to mitigate risks. It calls for researchers and developers to give serious consideration to the dual nature of their work and the risks that it might lead to. It highlights the need for best practice and involvement of a range of stakeholders and domain experts in the discussion.

The good news is that we can develop good AI to fight the bad. For example, AI is already being used to provide predictive and preventive cyber protection for enterprise systems. However, we cannot ignore the threat of malicious AI and must act to prevent it effectively.

Governments are starting to act; significant strides have been made by the European Union (EU) and, to some degree in the United States. The EU has taken a leading role with the recent adoption of its AI Act. This is comprehensive legislation that covers various aspects of AI use, including transparency, biometric surveillance, and regulation of high-risk AI systems. In the US, federal- and state-level actions reflect a growing focus on AI governance. President Biden's recent Executive Order emphasises safe, secure and trustworthy AI development. Several states, including Colorado and Illinois have enacted or proposed AI-related laws. These laws address issues from AI in hiring processes to AI-generated content disclosures in political ads.

In the UK in March 2023 the Conservative Government proposed an AI regulation white paper, emphasising a proportionate and pro-innovation approach to AI governance. New initiatives are likely to follow from the Labour Government, which came into office following the UK's general election in July 2024.

China continues to enhance its regulatory framework, focusing on ethical guidelines and national security implications of AI.

Common themes

While there are differences in approach, there are many common themes emerging in global AI legislation:

- Risk-based approach: Many countries are adopting a risk-based approach, with stricter regulations for high-risk AI applications, for example when used in critical infrastructure.

- Transparency and accountability: There is a growing emphasis on transparency in AI algorithms and decision-making processes, as well as accountability for potential harms caused by AI systems.

- Human oversight: The importance of human oversight and control over AI systems is increasingly recognised.

- Ethical considerations: Considerations such as fairness, non-discrimination and privacy are becoming more prominent in AI legislation.

While these legislative efforts represent significant progress, they face criticisms regarding enforceability and potential stifling of innovation. Nonetheless, these regulations are crucial in ensuring responsible AI development and mitigating associated risks.

Overall, as AI technology continues to evolve, so too will the legislative frameworks aimed at regulating its development and use, balancing innovation with the need for accountability and safety. The industry is starting to act too. For example, guidance is emerging from institutions such as the Institute of Electrical and Electronics Engineers (IEEE) in the US. The latter has developed the IEEE CertifAIEd program (2024), a certification initiative aimed at assessing the ethical implications of autonomous intelligent systems (AIS). This programme helps organisations ensure their AI systems are trustworthy and adhere to ethical standards. Key focus areas are transparency, accountability, algorithmic bias and privacy. The certification process involves a thorough review and independent verification to certify compliance with these ethical criteria.The Future of Life Institute published the 'Asilomar AI principles' back in 2017 (Future of Life Institute, 2017). These are 23 guiding principles for AI development and application.

Software tools and methodologies to help remove bias from algorithms are also emerging. These address aspects such as bias in data and personal data privacy. There are tools that check and certify AI software for cybersecurity resilience and protection against tampering and hacking.

This is an emerging field and much still needs to be done to educate the industry's workforce and to raise awareness about poor software development practices that can lead to problems in the finished product.

ETHICAL TECHNOLOGY

I believe strongly that we should take into account the ethics of technology as a whole, which receives much less attention than AI. For example, the majority of mobile phone users did not or still do not know about tracking and information sharing by apps. When Apple introduced its App Tracking Transparency to let users know, 85 per cent said no to tracking (Appleyard, 2021). This kind of tracking is not an AI problem but a bigger technology issue. Tracking of user activity is just one of the problems with seemingly harmless apps that billions of us have downloaded on our phones. Location tracking is particularly bad and has already started to eat into people's privacy in harmful ways. There is the case of the priest, a top US Catholic Church official, who was outed by the Catholic press when location tracking apps on his phone revealed that he was visiting gay bars. According to *The Washington Post* he had to resign (Boorstein et al., 2021). The consequences of such a capability enabled by a seemingly harmless app on a phone are huge. It is not just the loss of privacy but increased physical risks for people, for women with abusive partners for example.

This example illustrates one of the many reasons why we should work towards ethical technology and not just AI. This is why in 2020, at Emergence Partners, I created the Ethics in Technology Assessment (ETA) framework to help technology vendors assess the ethics in the development and features of their products to identify any gaps and risks, and plan remedial action.

AI FOR GOOD

The potential of AI for good should not be overshadowed by the possibility of its malicious use. I highlighted the use of AI to reduce energy consumption in industrial plants in Chapter 1. Another example in Chapter 5 was how AI is starting to help the elderly in their homes. AI to improve patient outcomes in stroke care was the subject of the RBFT case study in Chapter 8. These and more examples are highlighted in Figure 11.4.

Figure 11.4 Examples of AI for good

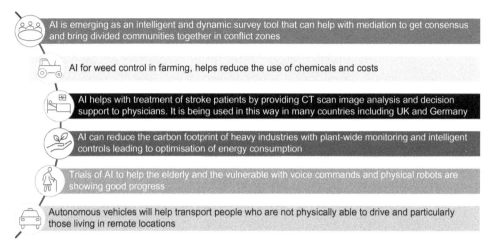

The examples that I have provided in Figure 11.4 contribute to achieving the United Nations' 17 Sustainable Development Goals (United Nations, n.d.). These include:

- zero hunger;
- good health and well-being;
- reduced inequalities;
- climate action;
- life on land;
- peace, justice and strong institutions.

We can accelerate the achievement of the goals with AI but must actively follow good risk mitigation strategies that include well-considered development using best practice and continuous monitoring and assessment of intelligent systems and their outcomes. In this way we can ensure that the development of AI is sustainable as well.

Another point is that it is through advances in AI for cybersecurity that we can fight its malicious use in cyber and political spheres. AI to find and highlight misinformation spread via social media is already being trialled, and more developments are sure to follow.

SUMMARY

The future of jobs is a very important issue that we need to address as enterprises become increasingly autonomous. While automation will reduce the number of jobs in some organisations, other forces are at work that will continue to fuel the jobs market.

Firstly, the ageing population indicates that vacancies will continue to increase in some industries. Secondly, insights from the UK ONS and government indicate the rising importance of skills, with many skilled vacancies proving hard to fill. Thirdly, another study by the ONS indicates that some low-skilled jobs are more likely to be automated than others. These findings point to the importance of helping people to gain the skills that are in demand to mitigate risks of unemployment.

History has shown us how, as some jobs disappeared over the centuries, new ones came about. That pattern is likely to continue in the future with demand for AI solutions creating new roles in its own right. Growing industries such as technology, space exploration and tourism are also set to create more demand for human workers.

Government and industry players are starting to address the issue of AI ethics. This is needed to ensure fair outcomes from AI. The risk from malicious uses of AI cannot be ignored. While good AI applications are being developed to counter some of the threats, more action is needed by governments and the industry to mitigate them.

I believe that the focus on ethics of AI alone is insufficient to address the bigger problem of ethics of technology as a whole, such as abuse of mobile phone data. The whole field needs to come under scrutiny, with good practice guidance provided and embedded across the industry.

These are exciting times for AI. We need to learn from our past mistakes, such as allowing unethical sharing and use of people's personal data by mobile apps, to guide AI development along an ethical path.

AFTERWORD

Since the publication of the first edition of this book in February 2022, the concept of the autonomous enterprise has gained increasing attention. Previously, the technology industry had not widely discussed this idea, as most organisations had only just started to invest in automation of knowledge work at scale. Many of the necessary technologies were still emerging back then. However, today's rapid advances in AI have provided a clearer vision of the future, validating my belief in the concept and the trajectory that I have outlined in the book.

As AI technology advances and levels of automation of office work increase, and the shift of focus from digital to phygital goes on, we will see more and more autonomous enterprises emerging, with work, real-life and virtual experiences being transformed over time.

We are already at the start of this journey, and it is important that we learn how best to make the trip, so we do not repeat the mistakes of the past. Personal data abuse fiascos have happened all too often because of the digitalisation of services, and new threats have been created, albeit inadvertently. If we can navigate this process well, we might be able to hand the Earth to future generations in a better state.

The way that we work will change, and this change needs to be managed to ensure resilient enterprises. Organisations will need to prepare for the change and be willing to adopt the new operating models that are likely to emerge with increasing enterprise autonomy. Furthermore, the ethics of AI need to be managed, and there is no time like the present for governments, the technology industry and users of technology to act to ensure that AI is developed and applied ethically and fairly. It is also important to develop good AI to mitigate the risks of its malicious use.

AI gives us great potential to innovate. In my mind, this is one of its most important aspects. Accordingly, my final recommendation to you is to go forth and innovate with AI.

I hope I have inspired you to examine the opportunities that are out there for your organisation and along the path to enterprise autonomy. I wish you all the best with your journey.

REFERENCES

Appleyard, B. (2021) Apple vs Facebook: Silicon Valley's new cold war. *New Statesman*, 16 July. p. 22.

Arnold, Z., Rahkovsky, I. and Huang, T. (2020) *Tracking AI Investment.* Washington DC: Center for Security and Emerging Technology. Available from https://cset.georgetown.edu/publication/tracking-ai-investment/

Blake, D. S. (2022) Using neural networks and deep learning to improve forecasting and availability. Ocado Technology Blog. 7 February 2022. Available from: https://medium.com/ocadotechnology/using-neural-networks-and-deep-learning-to-improve-forecasting-and-availability-803a2f111f68

Boorstein, M., Iati, M. and Shin, A. (2021) Top US Catholic Church official resigns after cell phone data used to track him on Grindr and to gay bars. *The Washington Post.* 21 July.

Bornet, P., Barkin, I. and Wirtz, J. (2020) *Intelligent Automation: Welcome to the World of HYPERAUTOMATION*. World Scientific Publishing Co.

Brainomix (2024) Voice of the physician. Vimeo. Available from: https://vimeo.com/961114901

Brundage, M. et al. (2018) *The Malicious Use of Artificial Intelligence: Forecasting, Prevention, and Mitigation*. Future of Humanity Institute, University of Oxford, Centre for the Study of Existential Risk, University of Cambridge, Center for a New American Security, Electronic Frontier Foundation, OpenAI.

Burnett, S. (2019) Five AI advancements that are making intelligent automation more intelligent. *Information Age.* 11 July. Available from www.information-age.com/intelligent-automation-sarah-burnett-14207/

Care at Home using Intelligent Robotic Omni-function Nodes (CHIRON) (2018) Available from https://chiron.org.uk/

Centre for Aging Better (2024) *Our Ageing Population | The State of Ageing 2023-24.* Available from https://ageing-better.org.uk/our-ageing-population-state-ageing-2023-4

Chui, M. et al. (2023) *The Economic Potential of Generative AI: The Next Productivity Frontier.* McKinsey Digital. Available from www.mckinsey.com/capabilities/mckinsey-digital/our-insights/the-economic-potential-of-generative-ai-the-next-productivity-frontier

Cockburn, I. M., Henderson, R. and Stern, S. (2018) *The Impact of Artificial Intelligence on Innovation*. National Bureau of Economic Research. Available from www.nber.org/papers/w24449

Dahlquist, E. (2020) Plant-wide monitoring and control of data-intensive processes with AI functions. Open Access Government. 2 October. Available from www.openaccessgovernment.org/plant-wide-monitoring-and-control-of-data-intensive-processes-with-ai-functions/95449/

Deep AI (n.d.) Glossary and terms: ReLu. DeepAI. Available from https://deepai.org/machine-learning-glossary-and-terms/relu

DeepMind (2020) Using Unity to help solve intelligence. London: DeepMind. Available from https://doi.org/10.48550/arXiv.2011.09294

European Court of Auditors (2024) *EU Artificial Intelligence Ambition: Stronger Governance and Increased, More Focused Investment Essential Going Forward.* Available from www.eca.europa.eu/en/publications?ref=SR-2024-08

European Union (2020) *White Paper on Artificial Intelligence: A European Approach to Excellence and Trust.* Brussels: European Union. Available from https://commission.europa.eu/publications/white-paper-artificial-intelligence-european-approach-excellence-and-trust_en

Eurostat (2022) Recent job starters by economic activity in the EU, Q3 2021. 22 October. Available from https://ec.europa.eu/eurostat/en/web/products-eurostat-news/-/ddn-20220304-1

Everest Group (2020) *Enterprise Intelligent Automation Adoption Maturity | Pinnacle Model Analysis.* Dallas: Everest Group.

Everest Group (2022) *Enterprise Intelligent Automation Adoption Maturity | Pinnacle Model Assessment.* Dallas: Everest Group.

Feng, J. and Shengnan, L. (2019) Performance analysis of various activation functions in neural networks. *Journal of Physics: Conference Series* 1237, 022030. Available from https://iopscience.iop.org/article/10.1088/1742-6596/1237/2/022030

Fisher, R. (2024) Gartner warns that GenAI 'will directly lead to the death of a customer' by 2027, *CX Today*, 22 February. Available from www.cxtoday.com/contact-centre/gartner-warns-that-genai-will-directly-lead-to-the-death-of-a-customer-by-2027/

Fortune Business Insights (2024) *Contact Center Software Market Size.* Fortune Business Insights. Available from www.fortunebusinessinsights.com/industry-reports/contact-center-software-market-100840

Future of Life Institute (2017) *Asilomar AI Principles.* Available from https://futureoflife.org/ai-principles/

Griffin, A. (2016) Tay tweets: Microsoft apologises for robot's racist and genocidal tweets. *The Independent.* 27 March. Available from www.independent.co.uk/life-style/gadgets-and-tech/news/tay-tweets-microsoft-apologises-for-robot-s-racist-and-genocidal-tweets-a6955056.html

Groette, O. (2024) What percentage of trading is algorithmic? (Algo Trading Market Statistics). Quantified Strategies, 7 April. Available from www.quantifiedstrategies.com/what-percentage-of-trading-is-algorithmic/

Health Innovation Oxford and Thames Valley (2023) Oxford stroke centre is among first to hit NHS target for key treatment, 25 September. Available from www.healthinnovationoxford.org/news-and-events/news/oxford-stroke-centre-is-among-first-to-hit-nhs-target-for-key-treatment/

HM Revenue and Customs (2020) *Personal Tax Credits Statistics: Child and Working Tax Credits Error and Fraud Statistics 2018–19, First Release.* Liverpool: HM Revenue and Customs.

IEEE CertifAIEd program (2024) Available from https://engagestandards.ieee.org/ieeecertifaied.html

Keras (n.d.) Getting started with Keras. Available from https://keras.io/getting_started/

Lee, C.-S. (2001) *An Analytical Framework for Evaluating E-commerce Business Models and Strategies.* Bradford: MCB University Press.

Lillicrap, D. G. (2018) *Measuring Abstract Reasoning in Neural Networks.* Stockholm: DeepMind.

Lowe, A. and Lawless, S. (2020) *Artificial Intelligence Foundations: Learning from Experience.* Swindon: BCS.

Mukerji, P. (2019) *The Impact of Algorithmic Trading in a Simulated Asset Market.* Basel: MDPI.

Nagaratnam, K. (2020) *Implementing AI in Stroke Pathway: Local and Regional Experience.* Presentation deck by Dr Kiruba Nagaratnam, Clinical Lead for Stroke Medicine, Royal Berkshire NHS FT, Clinical Lead (Acute), BOB ISDN, Reading.

National Audit Office (2019) *Local Government Finance and the 2019 Spending Review.* London: UK Parliament. Available from https://publications.parliament.uk/pa/cm201719/cmselect/cmcomloc/2036/203605.htm

National Audit Office (2024) *Local Government Financial Sustainability: Work in Progress.* Available from www.nao.org.uk/work-in-progress/local-government-financial-sustainability/

Ocado Group (2019) *Changing the Way the World Shops: Ocado Group plc Annual Report and Accounts. For the 52 Weeks Ended 1 December 2019.* Hatfield: Ocado Group.

Ocado Group (2023) *Solutions that Deliver, Innovations that Inspire: Ocado Group plc Annual Report.* Hatfield: Ocado Group.

Office for National Statistics (ONS) (2019) Which occupations are at highest risk of being automated? Office for National Statistics, 25 March. Available from www.ons.gov.uk/employmentandlabourmarket/peopleinwork/employmentandemployeetypes/articles/whichoccupationsareathighestriskofbeingautomated/2019-03-25

Office for National Statistics (ONS) (2024) VACS01: Vacancies and unemployment (dataset). Available from www.ons.gov.uk/employmentandlabourmarket/peoplenotinwork/unemployment/datasets/vacanciesandunemploymentvacs01

Open Access Government (2020) *The FUDIPO Project: AI Systems in Process Industries.* Open Access Government. Crewe, Cheshire: Adjacent Digital Politics Ltd. Available from www.openaccessgovernment.org/the-fudipo-project-ai-systems-in-process-industries/83756/

Pratt, M.K. and McLaughlin, E. (2023) Definition: Business innovation. TechTarget. Available from https://searchcio.techtarget.com/definition/business-innovation

Shead, S. (2021) UK aims to boost solar by predicting cloud movements with AI. CNBC Sustainable Future. 23 August. Available from www.cnbc.com/2021/08/23/uk-to-use-ex-deepmind-scientists-cloud-predicting-ai-to-boost-solar.html

Shumailov, I. et al. (2024) AI models collapse when trained on recursively generated data. *Nature*, 631. 755–759.

Slegers, J. (2022) Optimising the present, de-risking the future and discovering the intractable with digital twin simulations. Ocado Technology Blog, Medium, 28 January. Available from https://medium.com/ocadotechnology/digital-twin-simulations-optimising-the-present-de-risking-the-future-discovering-the-9059dabcd53

Stroke Association (n.d.) Signs and symptoms. Available from www.stroke.org.uk/what-is-stroke/what-are-the-symptoms-of-stroke

Thomas, D., Imtiaz, M. and Sabater, A. (2024) Private equity-backed investment surge in generative AI defies 2023 deal slump. S&P Global. Available from: www.spglobal.com/marketintelligence/en/news-insights/latest-news-headlines/private-equity-backed-investment-surge-in-generative-ai-defies-2023-deal-slump-80625128

UK Government (2019) *Policy Paper: AI Sector Deal*. London: UK Government. Available from www.gov.uk/government/publications/artificial-intelligence-sector-deal/ai-sector-deal

UK Government (2020) *Guidance – Trend Deck 2021: Skills*, June. Available from www.gov.uk/government/publications/trend-deck-2021-skills/trend-deck-2021-skills

United Nations (n.d.) *Sustainable Development Goals*. Available from www.un.org/sustainabledevelopment/

US Bureau of Labor Statistics (2024) Civilian unemployment rate. Available from www.bls.gov/charts/employment-situation/civilian-unemployment-rate.htm

Vaswani, A. et al. (2017) Attention is all you need. Available from https://doi.org/10.48550/arXiv.1706.03762.

Wärtsilä Corporation (2024) *Wärtsilä's Financial Statements Bulletin January–December 2023*. Available from www.wartsila.com/media/news/31-01-2024-wartsila-s-financial-statements-bulletin-january-december-2023-3396344

Williams, R. (2019) Fan Hui: What I learned from losing to DeepMind's AlphaGo. *i*. 25 May. Available from https://inews.co.uk/news/technology/fan-hui-what-i-learned-from-losing-to-deepminds-alphago-google-295005

Yee, L., Chui, M. and Roberts, R. (2024) *McKinsey Technology Trends Outlook 2024*, McKinsey Digital. Available from www.mckinsey.com/capabilities/mckinsey-digital/our-insights/the-top-trends-in-tech

FURTHER READING

Bornet, P., Barkin, I. and Wirtz, J. (2020) *Intelligent Automation: Welcome to the World of HYPERAUTOMATION*. World Scientific Publishing Co.

Burgess, A. (2018) *The Executive Guide to Artificial Intelligence: How to Identify and Implement Applications for AI in your Organisation*. Cham: Palgrave Macmillan.

Crawford, K. (2021) The *Atlas of AI: Power, Politics, and the Planetary Costs of Artificial Intelligence*. New Haven, CT: Yale University Press.

Pesce, M. (2023) *Getting Started with ChatGPT and AI Chatbots: An Introduction to Generative AI Tools*. Swindon: BCS Publishing.

Suleyman, M. and Bhaskar, M. (2023) *The Coming Wave*. London: Penguin Random House.

Willcocks, L. P. and Lacity, M. C. (2016) *Service Automation, Robots and the Future of Work*. Stratford upon Avon: Steve Brooks Publishing.

Wooldridge, M. (2020) *The Road to Conscious Machines: The Story of AI*. London: Pelican Books.

USEFUL WEBSITES

Alan Turing Institute
www.turing.ac.uk/

Amazon SageMaker
https://aws.amazon.com/sagemaker/

Apple machine learning research
https://machinelearning.apple.com/

Apple Neural Engine wiki
https://apple.fandom.com/wiki/ Neural_Engine

Facebook Prophet
https://facebook.github.io/prophet/

Google Cloud Model Garden
https://cloud.google.com/model-garden

Google Vertex AI on Google Cloud
https://cloud.google.com/vertex-ai/docs/start/introduction-unified-platform

IBM AI
www.ibm.com/cloud/learn/what-is-artificial-intelligence

Imperial College AI
www.imperial.ac.uk/computing/research/artificial-intelligence/

Keras
https://keras.io/

Microsoft AI
www.microsoft.com/en-gb/ai/experience-ai

MIT AI news
https://news.mit.edu/topic/artificial-intelligence2

Natural Language Toolkit
www.nltk.org/

NVIDIA Clara
www.nvidia.com/en-gb/clara/

OpenAI
https://openai.com/

Oxford University research on AI
www.ox.ac.uk/ai-oxford

PyTorch
https://pytorch.org/

TensorFlow
www.tensorflow.org/

University of Cambridge AI
www.cam.ac.uk/topics/Artificial-intelligence

ABBREVIATIONS

AI	artificial intelligence
API	application programming interface
BFSI	banking, financial services and insurance
BoM	bill of materials
BPM	business process management
CapEx	capital expense
CPQ	configure price quote
CRM	customer relationship management
CT/CTA	computerised tomography angiography
ERP	enterprise resource planning
EU	European Union
FTE	full-time equivalent
Gen AI	generative AI
HR	human resources
IA	intelligent automation
IDP	intelligent document processing
IoT	Internet of Things
IPA	intelligent process automation, often referred to as intelligent automation
IT	information technology
IVA	intelligent virtual agent/assistant
IVT	intravenous thrombolysis
JRH	John Radcliffe Hospital
KYC	know your customer
LLM	large language model
LVO	large vessel occlusion
ML	machine learning
MT	mechanical thrombectomy
NLG	natural language generation
NLP	natural language processing
NLU	natural language understanding

NPC	non-player character
OCR	optical character recognition
ONS	Office for National Statistics
OpEx	operating expense
P2P	Purchase to Pay
PO	purchase order
PoC	proof of concept
RBFT	Royal Berkshire NHS Foundation Trust
RDA	robotic desktop automation
ReLU	rectified linear unit
REST APIs	RESTful application programming interfaces
RoI	return on investment
RPA	robotic process automation
SLA	service level agreement
SSC	shared services centre
SSV	skill-shortage vacancy
TITAN	Thrombectomy Innovation and Transformation Network
UI	user interface
VIRA	Virtual, Interactive, Responsive Assistant

GLOSSARY

Anterior circulation: The blood supply to the front of the brain.

Application programming interface (API): An API allows software to connect to other software. It is a documented and standardised interface through which programs can connect and provide services to each other.

Artificial intelligence (AI): Refers to systems designed by humans that, given a complex goal, act in the physical or digital world by perceiving their environment, to build intelligent entities (Lowe and Lawless, 2020).

Attended automation: This is a term used in the field of robotic process automation to refer to robots that are activated by humans and that return controls to humans after completing their tasks (as opposed to being run according to predefined schedules or set off by events).

Banking, financial services and insurance (BFSI): The name for the financial services industry that includes banks and insurance companies.

Bill of materials (BoM): The complete list of materials and components used in making a product.

Business process management (BPM): The science of managing business processes and the software solutions that support it.

Capital expense (CapEx): Expenditure on capital items such as equipment, software and real estate.

Computer vision: The technology and techniques that allow machines to capture information from pictures, images, three-dimensional objects, scans, videos and other visual inputs.

Computerised tomography angiography (CT/CTA): A type of scanning of the human body that uses contrasting material injected into the blood to identify health problems with blood vessels and related diseases.

Configure price quote (CPQ): A category of software that allows sales teams to configure a product according to the customer's requirements and preferences, to allow them to estimate the price of the product to produce a quote.

Constraints inference: Understanding the consequences of constraints on automated decision-making.

Decision tree: A decision-support tool that models decisions and their consequences in the context of a specific business requirement, setting or scenario.

Diffusion model: A deep learning model that learns to generate data by reversing a gradual noising process, often used for high-quality image synthesis.

Digital twin: A digital twin is a virtual representation of a physical object or system that mimics the behaviour of that object or system, over a variable dimension such as time, using real-time data.

Enterprise resource planning (ERP): A group of software solutions to manage and run business processes including finance, supply chain and human resources.

Full-time equivalent (FTE): A unit used as a measure of the workload of a full-time employee.

Generative AI: Generative AI is a type of artificial intelligence that creates new content, such as images, text or music, by learning patterns from existing data and generating similar but original outputs.

Generative adversarial network (GAN): A deep learning framework where two neural networks, a generator and a discriminator, compete to create and identify realistic synthetic data.

Image recognition: A subset of computer vision, which classifies images.

Intelligent automation (IA): A term that describes a spectrum of software solutions that are used to automate business processes. These typically include a mix of intelligent and non-intelligent software such as chatbots and robotic process automation (RPA).

Intelligent document processing (IDP): A category of software that uses natural language processing (NLP) and other intelligent capabilities to automate processes that handle documents.

Intelligent process automation (IPA): Using intelligent automation software to automate business processes.

Intelligent virtual agent/assistant (IVA): Software that can process language, speech and text to offer services that would otherwise be provided by contact centre agents, or act as a virtual assistant to people.

Internet of Things (IoT): The network created as a result of devices and hardware being connected to the internet, therefore allowing humans and other devices to monitor them and the environment they are in and to communicate with them.

Intravenous thrombolysis (IVT): Delivery of drugs intravenously to eliminate blood clots that can form in the brains of stroke patients.

Ischaemic change: Changes to small blood vessels, in the context of this book, caused by lack of blood and oxygen after a stroke.

Knowledge work: Any work that primarily involves expertise to create, apply and deliver the products and services of an organisation.

Know your customer (KYC): A regulatory requirement in financial services to authenticate the identity of customers as part of offering them services.

Large language model: A model that is trained on very large volumes of textual information as the basis for generative AI with a focus on language.

Large vessel occlusion (LVO): Large blood clot.

Line of business: Refers to processes through which a business earns its revenue.

Mechanical thrombectomy (MT): A procedure to remove large blood clots from the brains of stroke patients.

Natural language generation (NLG): The techniques applied in software to generate words and sentences and interact with humans through natural languages by processing unstructured data.

Natural language processing (NLP): Techniques used in computing to process language. It has two primary components: natural language understanding (NLU) and natural language generation (NLG), described below and above, respectively.

Natural language understanding (NLU): Techniques used to enable machines to understand natural language. A part of natural language processing (NLP), described above.

Neural network: An artificial network of neurons or nodes used for predictive modelling in artificial intelligence.

Optical character recognition (OCR): Technology that enables text in scanned images to be converted to machine-readable characters, and thus allowing documents to be processed electronically.

Phygital: Refers to the field of technology that aims to bring the digital and physical worlds together by offering services that flow from one into the other.

Posterior circulation: The blood supply to the back of the brain.

Process discovery: A field of software that helps organisations find information about their processes. A part of process mining described below. In more recent years it is often used to refer to tools that identify manual processes that can be automated using intelligent automation software.

Process mining: The use of software that mines data held in program logs to build a virtual view of how processes are run in the organisation, to capture information about them to allow organisations to improve and optimise the processes, and to provide reports with process insights.

Proof of concept (PoC): A proof of concept is a small project that is undertaken by organisations to test the feasibility of a particular idea, method or technology and its viability.

Purchase order (PO): Used in enterprise procurement to manage orders and invoices.

Purchase to Pay (P2P): The end-to-end process of procuring and receiving goods and services, and paying and accounting for them in business.

Rectified linear unit (ReLU): An activation function in neural networks.

RESTful application programming interfaces (REST APIs): These are connecting interfaces between computer programs that adhere to representational state transfer (REST) architecture, collectively referred to as RESTful APIs.

Return on investment (RoI): The quantitative benefits that you realise from investing in assets such as hardware and software, as a proportion of the cost of purchasing them, and having them built, installed and run.

Robotic desktop automation (RDA): A class of software solutions that are activated by a user to automate a process on their desktop and then return control to the user. It is a term that is often used interchangeably with 'attended automation'.

Robotic process automation (RPA): A class of software that automates processes by connecting to business systems through the user interface, and thus mimicking the way humans work, for example logging in to a system and entering new data into a field, filling in a form and pressing submit.

Service level agreement (SLA): The agreed level of service to be delivered by a team, business unit or external service provider or contractor.

Shared service centre (SSC): A shared service centre is a centralised unit that provides support services, such as finance, HR or IT, to multiple parts of an organisation, aiming to increase efficiency and reduce costs.

Symbolic AI: A branch of artificial intelligence that focuses on representing knowledge and reasoning using symbols and logic. These symbols are manipulated according to predefined rules to draw inferences and solve problems.

Task mining: Task mining captures and analyses user interactions such as keystrokes and mouse clicks, to provide process intelligence that is then used to optimise the efficiency of tasks that make up larger complex processes in enterprises.

Text analytics: The process of deriving information from text sources in computing.

Unattended automation: Automation that is activated by systems to run according to predefined schedules, timetables or events.

User interface (UI): This is the layer of software that is used for interacting with users, typically via a physical or soft keyboard, mouse, touchpad, touchscreen, joystick, pen, and voice and gesture commands.

Vision language model (VLM): A VLM is an AI model that combines visual and textual data to interpret, analyse and generate information from both inputs.

INDEX